Taxcafe.co.uk Tax Guides

Using a Company to Save Tax

By Nick Braun PhD

Important Legal Notices:

Taxcafe®
TAX GUIDE - 'Using a Company to Save Tax'

Published by:
Taxcafe UK Limited
67 Milton Road
Kirkcaldy
KY1 1TL
Tel: (0044) 01592 560081

17th Edition, August 2017

ISBN: 978-1-911020-20-2

Disclaimer
Before reading or relying on the content of this tax guide please read the disclaimer.

Disclaimer

1. This guide is intended as **general guidance** only and does NOT constitute accountancy, tax, investment or other professional advice.

2. The author and Taxcafe UK Limited make no representations or warranties with respect to the accuracy or completeness of this publication and cannot accept any responsibility or liability for any loss or risk, personal or otherwise, which may arise, directly or indirectly, from reliance on information contained in this publication.

3. Please note that tax legislation, the law and practices by Government and regulatory authorities (e.g. HM Revenue & Customs) are constantly changing. We therefore recommend that for accountancy, tax, investment or other professional advice, you consult a suitably qualified accountant, tax adviser, financial adviser, or other professional adviser.

4. Please also note that your personal circumstances may vary from the general examples given in this guide and your professional adviser will be able to give specific advice based on your personal circumstances.

5. This guide covers UK taxation only and any references to 'tax' or 'taxation', unless the contrary is expressly stated, refer to UK taxation only. Please note that references to the 'UK' do not include the Channel Islands or the Isle of Man. Foreign tax implications are beyond the scope of this guide.

6. All persons described in the examples in this guide are entirely fictional. Any similarities to actual persons, living or dead, or to fictional characters created by any other author, are entirely coincidental.

About the Author & Taxcafe

Dr Nick Braun founded Taxcafe in 1999, along with his partner Aileen Smith. As the driving force behind the company, they aim to provide affordable plain-English tax information for private individuals, business owners and professional advisors.

Over the past 17 years Taxcafe has become one of the best-known tax publishers in the UK and has won several prestigious business awards.

Nick has been a specialist tax writer since 1989, first in South Africa, where he edited the monthly *Tax Breaks* publication, and since 1999 in the UK, where he has authored several tax books including *Small Business Tax Saving Tactics* and *Pension Magic*.

Nick also has a PhD in economics from the University of Glasgow, where he was awarded the prestigious William Glen scholarship and later became a Research Fellow.

Contents

Contents (cont...)

Contents (cont...)

Introduction

Using a company could save you over £10,000 in tax *every year*...possibly over £40,000.

There are several reasons why companies are such powerful tax shelters.

While sole traders and partnerships pay income tax and national insurance on their profits, companies only pay corporation tax – and corporation tax rates are much lower than personal tax rates.

Companies currently pay corporation tax at just 19%, whereas most sole traders and partners who earn over £45,000 pay 42% income tax and national insurance. Those with income over £150,000 pay 47% tax.

A company paying tax at just 19% will therefore have a lot more money left over to reinvest and grow than a sole trader or partnership paying tax at 42% or 47%.

Companies will enjoy even bigger tax savings when the corporation tax rate is reduced to 17% in April 2020.

Company owners also have to pay income tax on most of the money they extract from their companies (typically as dividends) and the bad news here is that dividend tax rates were increased significantly on 6th April 2016.

However, as a company owner you have complete control over *how much* income you withdraw from your company. This gives you complete control over your personal tax bill, allowing you to avoid the higher tax rates that kick in when your income exceeds £45,000, £50,000, £100,000 or £150,000. Sole traders and partnerships cannot control their income tax bills in this way.

Nevertheless, the increase in dividend tax means that companies no longer deliver guaranteed tax savings in all circumstances. What matters is how much profit your company makes and what you do with those profits.

Some of the subjects covered in this guide include:

- All relevant tax changes made in the March 2017 Budget.
- A plain-English guide to how companies are taxed.
- Detailed examples showing the exact amount of tax **you** could save by using a company.
- How to avoid paying any national insurance as a company owner.
- A plain English guide to how dividends are now taxed with lots of examples.
- How company owners can increase their tax savings by tens of thousands of pounds by keeping money inside their companies.
- How to save thousands more in tax by bringing your spouse or partner into the company.
- How to protect your child benefit payments.
- How to pay just 10% capital gains tax when you wind up your company and extract profits, plus details of new anti-avoidance rules.
- The *non-tax* benefits and drawbacks of using a company.
- The benefits and drawbacks of owning multiple companies.
- How to incorporate an existing business, including how to avoid capital gains tax and stamp duty land tax.
- Future tax changes and proposals.

The guide also contains many useful tables that show the exact tax savings (and losses) that can be enjoyed by using a company at every profit level. These tables take account of all taxes: income tax, corporation tax, national insurance etc.

The guide also examines a variety of other important tax issues facing company owners, including:

- Pension contributions
- Motoring expenses
- Tax treatment of losses
- Selling or winding up the business
- Business property
- Borrowing money

There has been much speculation in recent years that the Government will end the significant benefits of using a company.

The increase in dividend tax rates went some way towards achieving this but forthcoming cuts to corporation tax have also increased the attractiveness of using a company.

Politicians and governments have come and gone and, while there have been numerous changes, using a company will still produce handsome tax savings in many situations.

Using This Guide & Limitations

This tax guide deals primarily with the 2017/18 tax year, which started on 6 April 2017 and finishes on 5 April 2018. There are references to other tax years, however it is important to emphasise that the tax rates and tax laws that will apply in future tax years are not known with any degree of certainty.

Tax rates and tax laws (including HMRC's interpretation of those laws) are continually changing. The reader must bear this in mind when reading this guide.

The aim of this guide is to explain in plain English the tax benefits and drawbacks of using a company. Please note that this is NOT supposed to be a do-it-yourself (DIY) tax planning guide. If you are thinking of setting up a company I strongly recommend that you obtain professional advice after reading this guide.

Furthermore, although the guide covers a fair amount of ground, it does not cover every possible scenario and angle. Businesses and their owners come in many different shapes and sizes, so it is possible that the information contained in this guide will not be relevant to your circumstances.

There are also non-tax factors that have to be considered when deciding whether or not to use a company and these may be as important or more important than the tax issues.

For all of these reasons it is vital that you obtain professional advice before taking any action based on information contained in this guide. The author and Taxcafe UK Ltd cannot accept any responsibility for any loss which may arise as a consequence of any action taken, or any decision to refrain from taking action, as a result of reading this guide.

Scottish Taxpayers

The vast majority of the information contained in this guide is relevant to Scottish taxpayers and there are many references to Scottish tax. However, unless stated to the contrary, all examples, tables, calculations and illustrations are based on the assumption that the taxpayer concerned is not a Scottish taxpayer.

Part 1

Non-Tax Benefits & Drawbacks

Chapter 1

Company Benefits

Although one of the most important reasons for setting up a company is to save tax, there are many other benefits which have nothing to do with cutting your tax bill. Although they are not the focus of this guide, it's worth mentioning them in brief:

Limited Liability Protection

In layman's language, this means that a company's owners and directors are not responsible for the company's debts and cannot be sued by outsiders.

If your company goes bust your *personal* assets are safe. You do, however, stand to lose the money you've invested in the company and any assets you've transferred to the company.

This legal protection comes about because a company and its owners are separate legal entities in the eyes of the law. In legal terms this is often known as the 'veil of incorporation', with the company providing a barrier separating its assets from the shareholders' personal assets.

In practice, much of the limited liability benefit will be taken away by cautious lenders and suppliers. For example, banks will usually not lend money to small companies unless the directors or shareholders provide personal guarantees.

Furthermore, the directors may be held personally liable for losses resulting from their own illegal acts or if they act negligently or beyond their powers.

Directors can be held personally liable for the company's debts if there has been wrongful trading, i.e. if they know or should have known that there was no reasonable prospect of the debts being repaid because the company is in financial trouble.

The courts may intervene and 'pierce the corporate veil', holding those who control the company personally responsible, if the company is used as a device to commit fraud or to escape legal obligations.

In the case of *Gilford Motor Co Ltd v Horne*, the former employee of a car company (Mr Horne) set up a new company in his wife's name in an attempt to circumvent a non-compete clause in his previous employer's employment contract. The court granted an injunction against Mr Horne and the new company because the new company was formed merely to mask his activities.

In another case, *VTB v Nutritek*, the court confirmed that the corporate veil can only be pierced in these circumstances when there is some 'impropriety'. The company's involvement in any impropriety will not by itself justify piercing the veil – the impropriety 'must be linked to use of the company structure to avoid or conceal liability'.

In summary, limited liability protection could prove useful when the business faces unexpected losses or legal liabilities but will not protect you in all circumstances.

Finally, it should be noted that limited liability status can also be obtained by using a limited liability partnership (LLP).

Sole Enterprise with Protected Assets

In 2016 the Orwellian sounding "Office of Tax Simplification" published a discussion paper exploring the merits of introducing something called a Sole Enterprise with Protected Assets (SEPA).

The idea is to introduce a business structure that allows self-employed individuals to protect their primary residence (their home) without having to operate through a company. It would have the same tax and accounting treatment as a sole trader.

Customers seeking redress would no longer be able to place a charging order on a house under the Charging Order Act 1986, unless the sole trader was criminally negligent.

Creditors would still be able to ask for a business loan to be secured against a residence, in which case the SEPA status would not protect the owner.

As with directors of limited companies, sole traders would still be personally liable if they were found guilty of fraud or other serious failures.

There are over three million self-employed business owners in the UK and over 700,000 non-employing limited companies, all of which represent the target market for a Sole Enterprise with Protected Assets, as well as small companies with just one or two employees.

The Office of Tax Simplification believes that a number of the simplest companies would prefer to operate as a Sole Enterprise with Protected Assets rather than as a company, providing they are given full disincorporation relief (i.e. no tax payable when assets are transferred out of the company).

A final report published in November 2016 concluded that the SEPA idea is worth pursuing, although we do not know if or when the Government will act on this proposal.

Enhanced Status

Trading as a company is often seen as more prestigious than trading in your own name. Many people will have more faith in a business called Joe Bloggs Limited rather than just plain Joe Bloggs. Of course, it makes virtually no difference in practice whether a business is incorporated or not.

Borrowing Money

Corporate status seems to be a positive factor in the eyes of some lenders and may make it easier to obtain credit from suppliers. However, in reality, a newly formed company will probably struggle to obtain credit or borrow money without personal guarantees from the directors/shareholders.

Sole traders rely on their own personal credit ratings if they wish to borrow money for the business. If the business owner's personal credit rating deteriorates, this will affect the ability of the business to borrow.

Companies have their own credit scores, however these take time to build. For example, a lender may wish to see several years' worth of accounts before handing over any money.

Companies may, however, find it easier than sole traders and other unincorporated businesses to raise funds by issuing shares in the company to new investors.

An unincorporated business also cannot raise a 'floating charge' over its assets, whereas a company can. (With a floating charge the lender's claim is lodged over all of the assets, both present and future, rather than one specific asset. This leaves the borrower free to sell, buy and vary the assets within the group.)

Equity finance is also available to companies and there are schemes such as the Enterprise Investment Scheme (EIS) and Seed Enterprise Investment Scheme (SEIS) that can provide tax relief to the providers of the finance.

Flexibility of Ownership

Using a company makes it easy to involve new people in the ownership of the business and to separate ownership and management. If you want to involve your adult children or key employees, you can issue them with shares. Using a company allows you to provide small parcels of ownership quite easily.

If you want to keep your stake in the business but do not want to be involved in its management, you can keep your shares but resign as a director.

Similarly, passing the business on to family members can be easier if you use a company as you can leave shares to a number of different beneficiaries.

There are specific tax reliefs available for transferring shares in trading companies (but not investment companies). Therefore if you want to involve younger family members in the business you can frequently transfer shares to them free of UK tax by taking advantage of the various tax reliefs.

Continuity

It's something almost nobody setting up a business thinks about but is probably the most important decision facing business owners close to retirement: succession.

A company structure allows for a smooth exit from the company. Small parcels of shares can be passed on to family members over a number of years.

The death of a company member does not affect the existence of the company.

Chapter 2

Company Drawbacks

Using a company is not always in your best interests and it's worth pointing out some of the non-tax drawbacks (tax drawbacks are covered throughout):

Costs

It costs very little to set up a company. All you have to do is go to one of the many company formation experts and they'll do most of the work for just a few hundred pounds (although a more customised set up is more expensive).

Where you will incur higher costs is in *ongoing* accountancy fees. Most accountants charge companies more than sole traders and many partnerships because of the extra requirement to prepare and file accounts with Companies House.

Company accounts need to be filed in a prescribed format and have to be prepared in accordance with various financial reporting standards.

Accounts must be filed within 9 months of the end of the company's financial year and there are penalties for late filing. Filing accounts will also reveal financial information about your company.

In some cases the cost of preparing accounts will eat up the potential tax savings that can be enjoyed by using a company.

Fortunately, most small companies no longer have to undergo expensive and time-consuming audits of their annual accounts. For periods beginning on or after 1 January 2016 a company is considered small until it breaches any two of the following three thresholds for two consecutive financial years:

- An average of 50 employees
- £5.1 million gross assets
- £10.2 million turnover

Directors' Responsibilities

As a company director you have powers and responsibilities. There are serious penalties if you abuse those powers or fail to meet your responsibilities.

Every private company must have at least one director. Directors can be shareholders or company employees but this is not a requirement. Appointments and resignations must be reported to Companies House within 14 days.

Non-executive directors have the same legal duties, responsibilities and potential liabilities as the executive directors. Non-executive directors are not part of the executive management team and their main function is to provide objective criticism to the other directors.

Even if you are not a director, you could still be classed as a "shadow" director or "de facto" director if the other directors follow your instructions or if you, for example, resign and continue to act as a director.

Some people are not allowed to be directors, including those under 16, undischarged bankrupts and those who have been disqualified. You could be disqualified from being a director if you continue to trade when the company is insolvent or if you fail to keep proper accounting records and pay tax.

Directors have to comply with the company's articles of association, which set out how the company is to be run and how decisions are to be taken, for example how many directors are needed to vote on certain matters. These days most companies do not face too many restrictions relating to their activities.

Directors must also act in a way that is most likely to promote the success of the company for the benefit of its shareholders, having regard to the interests of the company's employees, the impact of the company's operations on the community and the environment, the long-term consequences of decisions and their effect on the company's reputation.

Consideration must also be given to the interests of all shareholders (although in practice the interests of minority shareholders are often overlooked).

Directors also have a duty to exercise reasonable care, skill and diligence. Directors are expected to behave in a way that can reasonably be expected from a person charged with those responsibilities. A director with a certain level of skill and experience will also be expected to act in a way that can reasonably be expected from someone with that level of knowledge.

Directors are not allowed to profit privately at the company's expense and must declare any conflict of interest, for example interests in other firms with which the company does business.

Directors must also make sure the company complies with its statutory filing responsibilities, including filing annual accounts, an annual return (now known as the annual confirmation) and appointments and resignations of directors and company secretaries. Failure to do this can result in fines, becoming disqualified from being a company director and even a criminal conviction.

Amongst other things, company directors must also comply with employment law and health and safety law. Directors can be personally sued for unfair dismissal and unfair work practices and for accidents caused by their negligence.

Recent Changes to Company Law

A number of changes have come about thanks to the Small Business, Enterprise and Employment Act 2015.

Companies must now check and confirm the information held about them at Companies House (known as a confirmation statement) instead of having to file an annual return. In practice there isn't a huge amount of difference between the old annual return and the new confirmation statement because most companies filed their annual returns online anyway and simply confirmed the pre-populated fields on the form.

One addition is that companies now have to provide information on "people with significant control". This is designed to increase the transparency of UK businesses by creating a publicly accessible register of who owns and controls UK companies.

Until recently companies had to maintain a number of statutory registers, which were open to inspection at their registered offices or another location which was provided to Companies House.

From 30 June 2016 private companies can elect to keep all their information on the public register at Companies House, instead of holding their own statutory registers of shareholders, directors (and their residential addresses) and people with significant control.

Although this should make life simpler for many small companies, one drawback is that information held at Companies House will be more easily accessed by the public (e.g. directors' dates of birth).

Recent Changes to Accounting Rules

A new financial reporting standard has been introduced (FRS 102) that sets the rules for how companies prepare their accounts.

Providing the shareholders approve, small companies have the option to prepare abridged rather than full accounts.

For periods beginning on or after 1 January 2016 small companies no longer have the option to file an abbreviated version of their full accounts with Companies House. However, they do have the option not to file the profit and loss account and the directors' report.

Different rules apply to "micro entities" which satisfy two of the following criteria for two consecutive financial years:

- Turnover no more than £632,000
- Gross assets not more than £316,000
- No more than 10 employees on average

Micro entities are permitted under the FRS 105 reporting standard to prepare simpler micro entity accounts.

A good accountant will be up to speed with these changes when it comes to drawing up accounts correctly. However, company directors themselves will have to ensure their actions are FRS 102/105 compliant to obtain the desired tax treatment in certain circumstances.

PAYE

PAYE applies to any business that has employees and therefore affects both limited companies and unincorporated businesses. The difference between companies and sole traders is that the sole trader himself will not be a salary earner and is therefore not subject to PAYE.

In a small company setting, the chances are that the owners of the business will also be directors and therefore PAYE may need to be deducted from any salaries paid to them, with the added requirement to operate the notoriously burdensome 'RTI' (real time information) procedures for payroll purposes.

An accountant or payroll provider can do all the work for you but you will probably end up paying at least a couple of hundred pounds per year for even the smallest husband and wife company.

Auto Enrolment

For several years now the Government has been rolling out a system of compulsory pensions called auto-enrolment. Essentially it's an extra tax on employers.

Only employees earning more than £10,000 and aged from 22 to state pension age need to be *automatically* enrolled into a pension. Some older and younger employees and those who earn less than £10,000 also have certain workplace pension rights.

According to the Pension Regulator a company does not have any automatic-enrolment duties when:

- It has just one director, with no other staff

- It has a number of directors, none of whom has an employment contract, with no other staff

- It has a number of directors, only one of whom has an employment contract, with no other staff

A contract of employment does not have to be in writing. However, according to the Pension Regulator, if there is no written contract of employment, or other evidence of an intention to create an employer/worker relationship between the company and the director, it will not argue that an employment contract exists.

If a director does not have an employment contract they are always exempt from automatic enrolment. If a director has a contract of employment and there are other people working for the company with an employment contract, they are not exempt.

Depending on their age and earnings, they may qualify for automatic enrolment but the company can decide whether to automatically enrol them into a pension. However, the director has the right to join a pension scheme at any time and the company cannot refuse to enrol them (although in practice this problem will not arise in most owner-managed companies).

If the company decides not to enrol any employed director who is eligible for automatic enrolment, and it has no other eligible staff, it does not need to set up a pension scheme. However, it will need to make a 'declaration of compliance'.

Part 2

Why Companies Are Excellent Tax Shelters

Chapter 3

Why You and the Company Aren't Really Separate

This is the shortest chapter in this guide but the message is an important one.

Although you and your company are separate legal entities, it always amazes us how many authors write about companies and their owner/managers as if they are completely separate. What nonsense!

As a company owner you care very much about how the company's money is spent. It is in reality – no matter what the textbooks say – YOUR money.

As a shareholder you have the ultimate say as to whether it goes to pay for your holiday or is simply given away to charity. Nobody else can tell you what to do with the company's money except in very exceptional circumstances.

In practice, therefore, you and your company are not really separate.

Why are we even mentioning this? Because throughout this guide, when we compare the tax treatment of companies and unincorporated businesses, we are interested in the **whole** picture.

We do not just look at the company's tax position in isolation from you, the shareholder/director.

We also do not look at your personal tax in isolation from the company's tax bill. We look at both as a single unit. This is the only way to compare doing business through a company with doing business as a sole trader or partnership.

Doing something that decreases your personal tax bill is not much use if it has an adverse effect on the company's tax position. It's your company, so in reality the company's tax bill is your tax bill.

Although there are special tax and other laws that affect you and the company differently, ultimately your aim is to use these to best advantage to improve your personal financial position.

There are many detailed examples of tax savings in this guide. Note that all of these examples take into account the tax position of both the company and its owners. So we may be including many taxes in the mix: corporation tax, income tax, capital gains tax and national insurance.

Chapter 4

Company Tax Basics

When it comes to tax, the most important difference between companies and other businesses can be summarised as follows:

Self-employed businesses (sole traders and partnerships) pay <u>income tax</u> and <u>national insurance</u> on their profits and <u>capital gains tax</u> on their capital gains.

Companies pay <u>corporation tax</u> on both their income and capital gains.

In this chapter I will explain how corporation tax is calculated. Despite all the mumbo-jumbo in tax textbooks, it's actually quite simple in most cases. In Chapter 7 we'll look at how sole traders and partnerships are taxed and in later chapters we'll compare the tax paid by company owners and the self employed.

Corporation Tax Rates

For the current financial year, which started on 1 April 2017, all companies (except some in the oil and gas sector) pay corporation tax at the same flat rate of 19%. The rate was previously 20%.

Things weren't always this simple. There used to be two headline corporation tax rates: a higher rate for companies with profits over £1.5 million (known as the 'main rate') and a lower rate for companies with profits under £300,000 (the 'small profits rate').

There was also a third rate applying to profits between £300,000 and £1.5 million.

Not only has corporation tax become a lot simpler, it has also been significantly reduced, as the Government has tried to boost the UK as a business destination. Back in 2007 the main rate was 30%.

Smaller companies haven't enjoyed such significant tax cuts, although it must be remembered that the small profits rate was due to rise to 22% back in 2011.

Future Changes to Corporation Tax

The corporation tax rate will be cut again to 17% on 1 April 2020.

In their 2017 election manifesto the Conservatives reaffirmed that this cut will take place: *"we will stick to that plan, because it will help to bring huge investment and many thousands of jobs to the UK"*.

Most small company owners will welcome these cuts because they will partly offset increases in the tax paid on the dividends they withdraw from their companies (see Chapter 10).

Northern Ireland

In Northern Ireland the rate is expected to be cut to 12.5% when corporation tax powers are devolved to the Northern Ireland Assembly.

This will bring Northern Irish companies in line with those in the Republic, making Northern Ireland a tax haven within the UK.

Corporation tax powers were originally expected to be transferred from April 2018 but this date has been put in doubt by the collapse of the Northern Ireland Government.

The recent Conservative and DUP Agreement on financial support for Northern Ireland contains the following statement on corporation tax: *"The UK government notes that one of the first tasks for the new Executive will be to work towards the devolution of Corporation Tax rates, the timetable for its introduction, and how this might best be flexibly managed, with options being developed for Autumn Budget 2017."*

So which companies/activities will qualify for the special tax rate when it is introduced?

The special corporation tax rate will apply to trading profits only. Other types of income, including investment income and property rental income, will be subject to the UK main rate of corporation tax, as will capital gains.

Micro, small or medium-sized enterprises (SMEs) will pay tax at the special rate on all their trading profits if they qualify as a

'Northern Ireland employer', i.e. if at least 75% of their staff time and costs relate to work carried out in Northern Ireland.

SMEs are currently defined under EU regulations as businesses with fewer than 250 employees and turnover of less than €50 million or a balance sheet total of less than €43 million.

Larger companies, with activity in both Northern Ireland and the rest of the UK, will have to treat their Northern Ireland trading activity as a separate business and allocate profits appropriately. The special rate will apply to profits that relate to the Northern Ireland trading presence, defined as a 'Northern Ireland regional establishment' (generally speaking a fixed place of business).

Legislation is being introduced to allow SMEs which do not qualify as Northern Irish employers, but do have a Northern Ireland regional establishment, to elect to use the large company rules to identify profits to which the Northern Irish tax rate applies. Otherwise they would not be able to benefit from the lower rate.

Look through Taxation Quashed

In 2016 the Office of Tax Simplification (OTS) investigated a system of "look through" taxation for small companies.

A look through system, if made compulsory, would take away the tax benefits of using a company. Under look through taxation, instead of paying corporation tax, the affected company owners would pay income tax and national insurance on all the profits of the business, just like sole traders and partnerships do.

As we shall see in Part 6, the advantage of using a company is that you can smooth your income and control your income tax bill by paying yourself dividends as and when you like.

Furthermore, those who wish to grow their businesses or protect themselves from a downturn can retain profits inside the company, in which case the only tax payable is 19% corporation tax (falling to 17% in 2020).

Fortunately, the OTS has decided not to recommend look through taxation because it would not simplify the tax system and harm investment. For now this specific threat has gone away.

Accounting Periods vs Financial Years

A company's own tax year (also known as its 'accounting period') may end on any date, for example 31 December, 31 March etc.

Corporation tax, on the other hand, is calculated according to financial years. Financial years run from 1 April to 31 March. The 2017 financial year is the year starting on 1 April 2017 and ending on 31 March 2018.

This matters when it comes to calculating how much tax your company will pay if the corporation tax rate has changed.

For example, on 1 April 2017 the corporation tax rate fell from 20% to 19%. A company whose accounting period runs from January 2017 to December 2017 will therefore pay corporation tax as follows:

- 3 months to 31 March 2017   20%
- 9 months to 31 December 2017   19%

The practical effect is that the company will pay 20% corporation tax on approximately one quarter of its profits and 19% tax on three quarters of its profits. (It doesn't matter at what point during the financial year the profits are actually made.) This means the company's effective corporation tax rate will be 19.25%.

A company whose accounting period runs from 1 August 2016 to 31 July 2017 will pay corporation tax as follows:

- 8 months to 31 March 2017   20%
- 4 months to 31 July 2017   19%

Thus the company will pay 20% corporation tax on two thirds of its profits and 19% tax on one third of its profits. This means the company's effective corporation tax rate will be 19.67%.

A company whose accounting period runs from 1 April 2017 to 31 March 2018 will simply pay 19% corporation tax on all of its profits.

Please note, in most of the corporation tax calculations in this guide we use the current headline 19% rate. This keeps things simple.

Chapter 5

Owning More than One Company: Benefits & Drawbacks

Company owners often think about setting up a second company, to keep a new venture separate from an existing business.

Often there are sound commercial reasons for using more than one company, including to:

- Limit liability
- Involve different shareholders
- Enable a stand-alone sale of the new business

For example, someone who owns an ecommerce business and a restaurant chain may wish to keep them separate so that each company can be sold more easily in the future.

Someone who owns a software company and a property rental business may wish to keep them in separate companies so that the 'trading' business (the software company) is not contaminated by the 'non-trading' business (the property rental business).

Companies that own non-trading assets, like rental property, can lose important tax reliefs, including Entrepreneurs' Relief, Holdover Relief and Business Property Relief.

Business owners used to be punished for owning more than one company. This is no longer the case (since April 2015).

What happened was the £300,000 small profit band (where the lower corporation tax rate was payable) had to be divided up among associated companies. For example, in the case of two companies, each company would start paying corporation tax at the higher rate when its profits exceeded £150,000 (instead of £300,000).

The associated company rules prevented the profits of one business being artificially spread over more than one company to avoid the higher rates of corporation tax.

The associated company rules have become largely redundant with the introduction of a single flat rate of corporation tax for all companies, currently 19%. You are no longer penalised for owning more than one company – they all pay corporation tax at the same rate.

Example

Maz owns an insurance broker called Insure Clever Ltd. The company makes profits of £200,000 per year. Maz recently inherited £500,000 and decides to buy some rental properties. He works out that he will be better off investing through a company instead of personally and sets up a second company called Clever Property Ltd (see the Taxcafe guide Using a Property Company to Save Tax *for a full discussion of this topic).*

Before April 2015, Maz would have been penalized for owning two companies. Insure Clever Ltd's small profit band would have been reduced from £300,000 to £150,000 and the company would have paid corporation tax at the higher rate on £50,000 of its profits.

But if instead Maz decided to stick with one company and use Insure Clever to buy the properties, it's possible he would have lost his entitlement to various tax reliefs like Entrepreneurs Relief.

Now, however, Maz can keep his insurance and rental property interests separate without suffering a higher corporation tax bill. Both companies will pay 19% tax on all their profits.

Although the associated company rules are no longer relevant when it comes to determining the corporation tax rate your companies pay, they're still relevant for other purposes, for example in deciding whether a company has to pay corporation tax in quarterly instalments. Instalments are generally payable by companies whose profits exceed £1.5 million but this amount is divided up if there are any associated companies.

Whereas small companies currently only have to pay their corporation tax nine months after the financial year has ended, companies subject to instalments have to start paying tax half way through the year.

The associated company rules have also been simplified with effect from 1 April 2015. From this date a new '51% group test' applies.

For example, if a company owns 51% of the share capital of three subsidiaries, all four companies will be associated. The £1.5 million profit limit would then be divided by four to determine whether each company has to pay corporation tax in instalments.

In the past the fact that Maz owns 100% of both Insure Clever Ltd and Clever Property Ltd would have meant that the companies were associated. However, under the new rules the fact that the ownership link is an individual doesn't count, i.e. the companies are not associated.

So some companies which previously were subject to the quarterly instalment regime may now find themselves outside it.

£3,000 Employment Allowance

Most businesses qualify for the employment allowance, which provides a saving of up to £3,000 per year in employer's national insurance.

However, a company cannot claim the employment allowance if a 'connected company' already claims it. Companies are connected if one company has control of the other company or both companies are controlled by the same person.

A person is generally considered to have control of a company if they hold more than 50% of the company's share capital or voting power or if they are entitled to more than 50% of the company's distributable income or assets if the company is wound up.

For example, if you own all the shares in two companies you will only be entitled to one employment allowance, even if the two companies are completely separate businesses with, for example, separate premises and staff.

If the company that claims the employment allowance has employer's class 1 national insurance of less than £3,000, the balance cannot be claimed by the other company.

Where there is 'substantial commercial interdependence' between two or more companies the holdings of close relatives and other 'associates' are added together to determine whether they are controlled by the same person or group of persons.

For example, if you own all the shares in company X and your spouse owns all the shares in company Y, your spouse's holding in company Y is attributed to you and you are treated as controlling company X and Y, as is your spouse. However, the two companies will only be treated as connected companies if there is substantial commercial interdependence between them.

If the two companies are completely unrelated then two employment allowances can be claimed. If there is substantial commercial interdependence between the companies then only one allowance can be claimed.

The definition of associates is broad but would typically include spouses, parents and grandparents, children and grandchildren, brothers and sisters, business partners and certain trusts.

To determine whether there is substantial commercial interdependence between two companies one or more of the following must be present:

- **Financial interdependence** – Two companies are financially interdependent if one gives financial support to the other or each has a financial interest in the same business.

- **Economic interdependence** – Two companies are economically interdependent if they have the same economic objective or the activities of one benefits the other or they have common customers.

- **Organisational interdependence** – Two companies are organisationally interdependent if they have common management, employees, premises or equipment.

Finally, please note that throughout this guide, the focus is mainly the tax position of a single trading company with no active associated companies.

Chapter 6

Trading Companies versus Investment Companies

In tax jargon a 'trading' company is one involved in, for want of a better word, 'regular' business activities, e.g. a company that sells goods online, a catering company or a firm of garden landscapers. Common types of non-trading company include those that hold substantial investments in property or financial securities or earn substantial royalty income.

Corporation Tax

Up until recently, if your company was engaged mainly in non-trading activities it would have been punished with a higher corporation tax rate. This is because a company classed as a close investment holding company (CIC) was not able to benefit from the lower small profits rate. It was forced to pay corporation tax at the main rate on all of its profits.

For example, if you set up a company to buy and sell stock market shares, a few years ago it would have been taxed at 30% (the main rate of corporation tax), even if it only made a small amount of profit.

Companies that own rental property were always excluded from the CIC provisions and were allowed to enjoy the lower small profits rate.

All this is no longer relevant because since April 2015 all companies, both trading companies and investment companies, pay corporation tax at the same flat rate – currently 19%.

Capital Gains Tax

If a company has too many non-trading activities (including most property investment and property letting) it may lose its trading status for capital gains tax purposes.

This will result in the loss of two important CGT reliefs:

- Entrepreneurs Relief
- Holdover Relief

Entrepreneurs Relief allows you to pay capital gains tax at just 10% when you sell your company shares, as opposed to up to 20%.

Holdover Relief allows you to give shares in the business to your children, common-law spouse and other individuals and postpone CGT. (You don't need Holdover Relief to transfer shares to your spouse because such transfers are always exempt.)

A company will only lose its trading status for CGT purposes if it has 'substantial' non-trading activities. To HMRC 'substantial' means more than 20% of various measures such as:

- Assets
- Turnover
- Expenses
- Profits
- Directors' and employees' time

HMRC may attempt to apply the 20% rule to any of the above measures.

Inheritance Tax

Shares in trading companies generally qualify for business property relief which means they can be passed on free from inheritance tax. However, if the company holds investments (including rental property) this could result in the loss of business property relief.

The qualification criteria are, however, more generous than for CGT purposes and a company generally only loses its trading status for inheritance tax purposes if it is 'wholly or mainly' involved in investment related activities.

To be on the safe side you may want to ensure that the company's qualifying activities exceed 50% of each of the measures listed above (e.g. turnover, time, profits etc).

For more information see our guide *How to Save Inheritance Tax*.

Incorporating an Existing Business

One of the key tax issues when incorporating an *existing* business is whether capital gains tax can be avoided or postponed when the business is transferred into the company. In general only trading activities qualify for capital gains tax deferral on incorporation. A non-trading activity may result in a significant tax bill.

Chapter 7

How the Self-Employed Are Taxed

Self-employed business owners (sole traders and partnerships) pay income tax and national insurance on their taxable profits:

Income Tax

For the current 2017/18 tax year most self-employed individuals pay income tax as follows:

- 0%   on the first   £11,500   Personal allowance
- 20%   on the next   £33,500   Basic-rate band
- 40%   above   £45,000   Higher-rate threshold

If you earn more than £45,000 you are a higher-rate taxpayer; if you earn less you are a basic-rate taxpayer.

In Scotland it's slightly different. You start paying 40% tax when your income rises above £43,000 – see below for further information.

Income over £100,000

When your income exceeds £100,000 your personal allowance is gradually reduced. It is reduced by £1 for every £2 you earn above £100,000. So once your income reaches £123,000 you will have no personal allowance left at all.

This is bad news for those earning over £100,000. The personal allowance currently saves higher-rate taxpayers £4,600 in tax.

Example
Bill has self-employment income of £110,000. His earnings exceed the £100,000 limit by £10,000. This means his personal allowance will be reduced by half this amount (£5,000), leaving him with a personal allowance of £6,500.

It's important to note that the £5,000 of income that was tax free will now be taxed at 40%, not 20%. The basic-rate tax band is limited to just £33,500 of income.

In summary, Bill pays income tax at the following rates:

First £6,500	*0%*
Next £33,500	*20%*
Next £70,000	*40%*

Paying Tax at 60%

Anyone earning between £100,000 and £123,000 faces a marginal income tax rate of 60%. This can be illustrated with the following example.

Example

Caroline, a sole trader, has earned taxable income of £100,000 so far during the current tax year.

If she receives an extra £100 of income she will pay an extra £40 of income tax. She will also lose £50 of her income tax personal allowance, so £50 of previously tax-free income will now be taxed at 40%, adding £20 to her tax bill.

All in all, she pays £60 in tax on her extra £100 of income, so her marginal income tax rate is 60%.

Income above £150,000

Once your taxable income exceeds £150,000, you will pay 45% income tax on any extra self-employment income. This is known as the additional rate of tax. It used to be 50%.

Self-employed taxpayers pay the same income tax as salary earners (including company owners who pay themselves salaries) but the national insurance position is different.

National Insurance 2017/18

Self-employed business owners pay class 4 national insurance as follows:

- 0%   on the first   £8,164
- 9%   on the next   £36,836
- 2%   above   £45,000

Those with earnings over the £6,025 small profits threshold also pay class 2 national insurance (£2.85 per week, £148 for the year) but this will be abolished from April 2018.

Certain types of income are not subject to national insurance, including interest from bank accounts (including business bank accounts) and rental income.

Combined Tax Rates 2017/18

Putting all of the above income tax and national insurance rates together, we can see that most self-employed business owners face the following combined marginal tax rates in 2017/18:

First £6,025	£0
£6,025 to £8,164	£148
£8,164 to £11,500	9%
£11,500 to £45,000	29%
£45,000 to £100,000	42%
£100,000 to £123,000	62%
£123,000 to £150,000	42%
Over £150,000	47%

Scottish Company Owners

The Scottish Parliament can now set the income tax rates and thresholds for most types of income, including self-employment income. It cannot, however, make changes to the income tax personal allowance or national insurance.

Any changes that make Scottish income tax more onerous will be suffered in full by *self-employed* business owners in Scotland. By contrast, as we shall see, Scottish *company owners* can shelter themselves completely from higher taxes north of the border.

For the current 2017/18 tax year the only difference between Scotland and the rest of the UK is the higher-rate threshold, which is £43,000 in Scotland and £45,000 in the rest of the UK.

As a result, self-employed business owners in Scotland who earn over £45,000 will pay £400 more income tax than self-employed business owners in the rest of the UK.

Future Changes to National Insurance

In the March 2017 Budget the Government tried to increase the rate of Class 4 national insurance from 9% to 11% by April 2019. Following a media backlash it was forced to perform an embarrassing u-turn and ditch the increase.

We at Taxcafe do not think a now weakened Conservative Government will attempt to reintroduce such an unpopular tax increase.

However, one cannot rule out any future government increasing Class 4 national insurance to level the playing field between the national insurance paid by employees and the self-employed.

Chapter 8

Companies as Tax Shelters

So which tax rates are better – the corporation tax rates outlined in Chapter 4 or the self-employment tax rates outlined in the previous chapter?

Let's say Joe Bloggs Limited has an accounting period that ends on 31st March 2018 and taxable profits of just £10,000. The company will pay £1,900 in corporation tax (£10,000 x 19%). But what if Joe Bloggs is a sole trader? Putting £10,000 into the table of combined tax rates in the previous chapter produces a tax bill of £313. The company's tax bill is £1,587 higher than the sole trader's.

Why? Companies pay corporation tax on ALL their profits, even if those profits amount to just a few hundred pounds. Sole traders, on the other hand, can currently receive up to £11,500 free from income tax and up to £8,164 free from class 4 national insurance.

Thanks to these tax-free allowances, when profits are low self-employed individuals pay less tax than companies.

However, when profits exceed £11,500, self-employed individuals start paying tax at 29%, which is more than companies pay.

The current threshold is roughly around £30,000: when profits are lower a company will pay more tax than a sole trader, when profits are higher a company will pay less tax than a sole trader.

When profits reach £45,000 the sole trader becomes a higher-rate taxpayer and starts paying tax at 42%, whereas the company continues paying tax at 19%. As a result, the savings from using a company start to accelerate.

For example, when profits reach £50,000 the company's tax bill will be £2,763 lower than the sole trader's and when profits reach £80,000 the company's tax bill will be £9,663 lower.

TABLE 1
Corporation Tax vs Sole Trader Tax 2017/18

Profits £	Corporation Tax £	Sole Trader £	Saving £
10,000	1,900	313	-1,587
20,000	3,800	2,913	-887
30,000	5,700	5,813	113
40,000	7,600	8,713	1,113
50,000	9,500	12,263	2,763
60,000	11,400	16,463	5,063
70,000	13,300	20,663	7,363
80,000	15,200	24,863	9,663
90,000	17,100	29,063	11,963
100,000	19,000	33,263	14,263
110,000	20,900	39,463	18,563
120,000	22,800	45,663	22,863
130,000	24,700	50,463	25,763
140,000	26,600	54,663	28,063
150,000	28,500	58,863	30,363
160,000	30,400	63,563	33,163
170,000	32,300	68,263	35,963
180,000	34,200	72,963	38,763
190,000	36,100	77,663	41,563
200,000	38,000	82,363	44,363
225,000	42,750	94,113	51,363
250,000	47,500	105,863	58,363
275,000	52,250	117,613	65,363
300,000	57,000	129,363	72,363
350,000	66,500	152,863	86,363
400,000	76,000	176,363	100,363
450,000	85,500	199,863	114,363
500,000	95,000	223,363	128,363
600,000	114,000	270,363	156,363
700,000	133,000	317,363	184,363
800,000	152,000	364,363	212,363
900,000	171,000	411,363	240,363
1,000,000	190,000	458,363	268,363

When profits reach £100,000 sole traders start losing their income tax personal allowance and when profits reach £123,000 the personal allowance will have completely disappeared. At this point a company will be paying over £24,000 less tax than a sole trader.

When profits reach £150,000 sole traders face their final attack, becoming additional-rate taxpayers who pay income tax and national insurance at the combined rate of 47%. By the time profits reach £200,000 this tax rate will have taken its toll and the company (still paying tax at 19%) will be paying £44,363 less tax than the sole trader.

If we bump the profits right up to £300,000, the company pays £72,363 less tax than the sole trader!

Table 1 compares corporation tax and self-employment tax at lots of different profit levels.

Unlike sole traders, companies pay tax at a flat rate – their tax rate does not increase as their profits increase. So a company with a profit of £1 million pays tax at the same rate as a company with a profit of £1,000.

What more incentive do you need to grow your business?

Should I Use a Company?

The message from Table 1 is NOT that businesses with profits over roughly £30,000 should operate as a company and vice versa. What I am trying to do in these early chapters is slowly build a picture of how company owners and sole traders are taxed.

The table doesn't look at the whole picture. Two things we have ignored are:

- Business owners with income from other sources

- The income tax paid by company owners when they extract income

Business Owners with Other Income

If you have income from other sources the sole trader tax bills listed in Table 1 may be too low.

For example, let's say you already receive income from a portfolio of rental properties and then decide to start a new business. If you set up a company to house the new business you will pay corporation tax on the profits at 19%, falling to 17% in April 2020.

However, if you operate as a sole trader you could end up effectively paying 40% income tax on your profits if your rental income is already using up your income tax personal allowance and basic-rate band. You may also end up paying 9% national insurance as well.

The bottom line: a company may be an excellent tax shelter if you have existing income from other sources and do not need to extract income from the company initially.

Profit Extraction = Additional Tax

For sole traders and partnerships there is no further tax to worry about once income tax and national insurance have been paid on the profits of the business. In other words, the numbers in Table 1 generally tell us the whole picture.

However, if company owners want to get their hands on the company's profits they have to pay themselves a salary or dividend. This usually results in more tax being paid.

The critical question is: After paying any extra tax will you be better off using a company? Answering this very important question is the main focus of this guide.

Reinvesting Profits

Although extra tax is usually payable when profits are withdrawn from a company via a salary or dividend, no extra tax has to be paid if profits are simply *reinvested*.

So the next important point to note is that:

Using a company is attractive if profits are reinvested.

Reinvesting profits may allow you to create a more valuable business that generates even higher income or can be sold for a significant sum at some point in the future.

Selling businesses is probably the most tax-efficient way to make a living in the UK. The proceeds are subject to capital gains tax and, if your company is a 'trading' company (rather than an investment company), you may qualify for Entrepreneurs Relief.

Entrepreneurs Relief allows up to £10 million of capital gains from the sale of businesses during your lifetime to be taxed at just 10%. The relief applies on a per person basis, so couples can have up to £20 million of gains taxed at 10%.

In effect, selling a business is a way of converting fully taxed income (future profits, salary, dividends etc) into capital gains that are taxed at a much lower rate.

Even if you decide not to sell your business, reinvesting profits will allow you to earn a higher income in the future, if done wisely.

Again using a company will add a great deal more powder to your keg. A company with £100,000 of profits will have around £14,000 more money left after tax than a sole trader. A company with £200,000 profits will have over £44,000 more money left after tax.

This money can then be spent on marketing, buying equipment, developing new products etc.

Of course, it's very unlikely that all of the profits of your business can be reinvested. If you want to pay yourself some income the incorporation question becomes a great deal more complex.

A whole host of factors come into play: how much of the company's profit you want to extract each year, whether to pay yourself a salary or dividends, the level of the company's profits and the tax-splitting opportunities available to you and your spouse or partner.

We will take a look at each of these factors in the chapters that follow.

Part 3

How Company Owners Can Pay Less Tax

Chapter 9

Employment Income

When HMRC and tax professionals talk about 'employment income', they are referring to salaries and bonuses.

These are subject to income tax and national insurance. They are also generally a tax-deductible expense for the company (i.e. they reduce the company's corporation tax bill).

Company owners pay the same income tax on their salaries as self-employed business owners (see Chapter 7). However the national insurance position is different: company owners pay 12% on earnings between £8,164 and £45,000, sole traders pay 9%.

Combined Tax Rates

As a result, the combined marginal rates of income tax and national insurance applying to salaries in 2017/18 are as follows:

Income up to £8,164   0%
Income from £8,164 to £11,500   12%
Income from £11,500 to £45,000   32%
Income from £45,000 to £100,000   42%
Income from £100,000 to £123,000   62%
Income from £123,000 to £150,000   42%
Income over £150,000   47%

Employer's National Insurance

There isn't a huge amount of difference between the tax paid by sole traders and the tax paid by company owners themselves on their salaries. However, we haven't looked at the BIG tax drawback of paying salaries yet: Employer's national insurance!

Most employees don't lose much sleep over their employer's national insurance bill. However, as a company owner, the company's money is effectively your money so this extra tax is an important consideration.

Companies currently pay national insurance at 13.8% on every single pound of salary the director earns over £8,164.

Employer's national insurance is, however, a tax-deductible expense for corporation tax purposes.

There is also the 'employment allowance' which reduces the national insurance paid by most companies by £3,000 per year. We'll return to this at the end of the chapter.

So what has all this got to do with the decision to start a company? If you start a company and take all your income as salary, you could end up paying a lot more tax than a sole trader.

Example

Margo is a sole trader with profits of £50,000 in 2017/18. We know from Table 1 that her total tax bill comes to £12,263, leaving her with an after-tax income of £37,737.

Richard owns a company that also makes profits of £50,000 (before deducting his salary and employers national insurance on that salary). Richard decides to extract all of the company's profits as salary. He doesn't pay himself £50,000 because he needs to leave enough money in the company to pay the employer's national insurance on his salary.

Instead he pays himself a salary of £44,927. The employer's national insurance comes to £5,073 – total cost £50,000. The company doesn't have any corporation tax to pay because the salary and employer's national insurance reduce its taxable profits to zero.

Richard himself will pay income tax of £6,685 and employee's national insurance of £4,412, leaving him with an after-tax income of £33,830.

In summary, the sole trader's total tax bill is £12,263. The company owner's total tax bill is £16,170 (including employer's national insurance). The company owner pays £3,907 more tax than the sole trader.

Table 2 shows the total tax paid by sole traders and company owners at different profit levels. In each case the company owner extracts all of the company's profits as salary. At all profit levels the company owner pays more tax than the sole trader.

TABLE 2
Company vs Sole Trader: All Company Profits as Salary

Profits £	Company Owner £	Sole Trader £	Tax Loss £
10,000	416	313	103
20,000	4,096	2,913	1,183
30,000	8,121	5,813	2,307
40,000	12,146	8,713	3,432
50,000	16,170	12,263	3,907
60,000	21,066	16,463	4,603
70,000	25,969	20,663	5,306
80,000	30,873	24,863	6,009
90,000	35,776	29,063	6,713
100,000	40,680	33,263	7,416
110,000	45,583	39,463	6,119
120,000	51,774	45,663	6,110
130,000	58,435	50,463	7,971
140,000	64,893	54,663	10,229
150,000	69,796	58,863	10,933
160,000	74,700	63,563	11,136
170,000	79,622	68,263	11,358
180,000	84,964	72,963	12,001
190,000	90,307	77,663	12,644
200,000	95,650	82,363	13,286
225,000	109,007	94,113	14,893
250,000	122,363	105,863	16,500
275,000	135,720	117,613	18,107
300,000	149,077	129,363	19,713
350,000	175,790	152,863	22,927
400,000	202,504	176,363	26,140
450,000	229,217	199,863	29,354
500,000	255,931	223,363	32,567
600,000	309,358	270,363	38,995
700,000	362,785	317,363	45,422
800,000	416,212	364,363	51,849
900,000	469,639	411,363	58,276
1,000,000	523,066	458,363	64,703

What Table 2 tells us is that if you run your business via a company, and take all your income as salary, you will not save any tax. In fact it could be a complete disaster. Your total tax bill could increase by thousands of pounds!

Although sole traders and company owners are subject to the same income tax rates on their earnings, they are subject to completely different national insurance systems.

This leads us to conclude that:

Using a company is a bad idea when all income is taken as salary.

Fortunately, as a company owner you do not have to take all your income as salary. You may also be able to pay yourself dividends. We will explain how dividends are taxed in the next chapter.

It's important to point out that not all company owners can pay themselves dividends. Under company law, a company cannot pay a dividend unless it has sufficient distributable profits to cover it. A company's distributable profits are its accumulated realised profits, less accumulated realised losses.

To determine whether a company has distributable profits it is necessary to prepare accounts, typically annual accounts. It may also be possible to prepare interim or management accounts to show there are sufficient profits to support a dividend.

However, one thing you cannot do is start a company and simply start paying yourself a dividend immediately, just because you don't want to pay yourself a heavily taxed salary. Dividends have to be supported by profits.

£3,000 Employment Allowance

Most businesses qualify for the employment allowance, which provides a saving of up to £3,000 per year in employer's national insurance.

Where a company has just a few low-paid employees, there may be spare employment allowance which will reduce the national insurance payable on the directors' own salaries.

A company with two directors (e.g. a husband and wife) and no other employees can pay the directors a salary of around £19,000 each with no employer's national insurance liability.

However, even with the £3,000 national insurance rebate, most sole traders will still pay less tax than company owners who withdraw all the profits as salary.

Furthermore, the employment allowance will not reduce the tax on the directors own salaries if it is used up paying salaries to other employees.

One Man Band Companies

Unfortunately the employment allowance is no longer available to "one man band" companies where there is just one director who is the only employee.

According to HMRC guidance, the employment allowance also cannot be claimed if there are other employees BUT the director's salary is the only one on which employer's national insurance is payable.

This is to prevent directors of one-man band companies employing friends or family and paying them a token amount in order to claim the employment allowance for their own salaries.

At least one of the additional employees must be paid more than the national insurance threshold. For example, a company that employs a seasonal worker who earns above the threshold in a week (£157 for 2017/18) will be eligible for the employment allowance for the whole tax year.

The second employee can be another director (e.g. your spouse) provided both directors' salaries exceed the *annual* threshold (£8,164 for 2017/18 or pro rata if the directorship begins after the tax year has started).

If circumstances change during the tax year and the director becomes the only employee paid above the secondary threshold, the employment allowance can still be claimed for that tax year.

It should be pointed out that several expert commentators,

including the Institute of Chartered Accountants, believe HMRC has not interpreted the law correctly and that it should be possible to claim the employment allowance even if the second employee receives a token salary on which no employer's national insurance is payable.

However, to be safe and avoid problems, it may nevertheless be necessary to pay a second employee a salary slightly higher than the national insurance threshold.

Scottish Company Owners

The Scottish Parliament can set the income tax rates and thresholds for salaries and most other types of income but not dividends or interest.

Thus a Scottish company owner who takes all or most of his income as salary will probably be subject to Scottish tax rates and thresholds... for better or worse.

For the current 2017/18 tax year the only difference between Scotland and the rest of the UK is the higher-rate threshold, which is £43,000 in Scotland and £45,000 in the rest of the UK.

Thus Scottish company owners whose salary and other income (except interest and dividends) is less than £43,000 will pay exactly the same amount of tax as taxpayers in the rest of the UK.

If your salary and other income (except interest and dividends) is more than £45,000 you will pay an extra £400 income tax this year.

Self-employed business owners in Scotland who earn more than £45,000 will also pay and extra £400 income tax this year.

However, as we shall see in the chapters that follow, Scottish company owners who take most of their income as dividends can completely escape the higher income tax that applies in Scotland.

Chapter 10

How Dividends Are Taxed

Company owners can avoid large national insurance bills by paying themselves dividends.

The important thing to note is that dividends are paid out of *profits*. If your company doesn't have any profits, it cannot pay you dividends.

Also, dividends are not a tax-deductible expense for the business. In other words, dividends are paid out of profits that have already been subjected to corporation tax. Salaries and bonuses, on the other hand, are tax-deductible expenses.

How Dividends Are Taxed

Because dividends are paid out of profits that have already been taxed in the hands of the company, the income tax rates on dividends are lower than for other types of income.

However, dividend tax rates were increased on 6 April 2016 (the start of the 2016/17 tax year). Dividend tax credits have also been abolished, so it is no longer necessary to gross up your dividends to calculate your tax. All tax calculations now work with "cash dividends" only and are therefore a lot simpler.

Currently the first £5,000 of dividend income you receive is tax free thanks to the "dividend nil rate band", also known as the "dividend allowance". Unfortunately, the dividend allowance will be cut to £2,000 in 2018/19.

For those receiving dividends in excess of the dividend allowance, the following income tax rates now apply (the old effective rates are included for comparison):

	Old	**Current**
Basic-rate taxpayers	0%	7.5%
Higher-rate taxpayers	25%	32.5%
Additional-rate taxpayers	30.6%	38.1%

Overall Tax Rates on Dividend Income

Because income paid out as dividends is taxed twice (first in the hands of the company and second in the hands of the shareholder) it's easy to lose sight of how much tax is being paid overall.

As a company owner you are likely to be equally concerned about your company's tax bill as your own, so it's worth showing the overall combined tax rate on dividend income.

With companies now paying 19% corporation tax, the total tax rates on dividend income are as follows:

	Total Tax Rate (rounded)
Basic-rate taxpayers	25%
Higher-rate taxpayers	45%
Additional-rate taxpayers	50%

For example, a company with £100 of profit will pay £19 corporation tax, leaving £81 to pay out as dividends. Ignoring the £5,000 dividend allowance, a higher-rate taxpayer will pay £26 tax on this income (£81 x 32.5%), so the total tax bill on the £100 profit is £45, which is 45%.

The above tax rates are higher than the regular income tax rates that apply to most types of income (20% for basic-rate taxpayers, 40% for higher-rate taxpayers and 45% for additional-rate taxpayers).

This is because the Government wants to level the playing field between company owners (who often don't pay any national insurance) and self-employed business owners and regular employees, who pay national insurance on most of their earnings.

The £5,000 Dividend Nil Rate Band

Company owners do not enjoy an additional standalone amount of £5,000 tax free. Instead, the dividend nil rate band typically uses up some of your basic-rate band.

If you have a £50,000 dividend and no other income, the first £11,500 will be tax free thanks to your personal allowance and the next £5,000 will be tax free thanks to the dividend nil rate band. Only £28,500 of your remaining income will be taxed at 7.5% because the £5,000 dividend nil rate band uses up part of your £33,500 basic-rate band. The final £5,000 will be taxed at 32.5%.

The dividend nil rate band only uses up your basic-rate band if, like many company owners, you have dividend income subject to basic-rate tax. It works differently if you have a lot of other income and all your dividends are subject to higher-rate tax.

The New Dividend Tax Regime – Examples

The taxation of dividends is best illustrated with some examples. To keep things simple, in each example we will assume that the company pays 19% corporation tax:

Example 1
Bob Limited makes a profit of £20,000. After paying corporation tax at 19% the company is left with after-tax profits of £16,200. Bob, the company's owner, pays himself a dividend of £16,200. He has no other taxable income.

The first £11,500 of Bob's dividend income is tax free thanks to his personal allowance and the next £4,700 is tax free thanks to the dividend allowance. Bob has no tax to pay personally, although his company faces a £3,800 corporation tax bill.

Example 2
Bob Limited makes a profit of £60,000. After paying corporation tax at 19% the company is left with after-tax profits of £48,600. Bob, the company's owner, pays himself a dividend of £48,600. He has no other taxable income.

The first £11,500 of Bob's dividend income is tax free thanks to his personal allowance and the next £5,000 is tax free thanks to the dividend allowance. The next £28,500 is taxed at 7.5% and the final £3,600 is taxed at 32.5%.

The total tax bill (including corporation tax) is £14,708 and Bob is left with an after-tax income of £45,292 (£60,000 - £14,708).

Example 3

Bob Limited makes a profit of £200,000. After paying corporation tax at 19% the company is left with after-tax profits of £162,000. Bob, the company's owner, pays himself a dividend of £162,000. He has no other taxable income.

Because Bob's income exceeds £123,000 his income tax personal allowance is taken away completely (see Chapter 7). And because his income exceeds £150,000 he is also an additional rate taxpayer.

The first £5,000 of his dividend income is tax free thanks to the dividend allowance, the next £28,500 is taxed at 7.5% and the next £116,500 at 32.5%. The final £12,000 is taxed at 38.1%. The total tax bill (including corporation tax) is £82,572 and Bob is left with an after-tax income of £117,428 (£200,000 - £82,572).

Company vs Sole Trader: All Income Taken as Dividends

Table 3 shows the total tax (corporation tax and income tax) payable by a company owner who takes all of his income as dividends. It also shows the total tax (income tax and national insurance) payable by a sole trader.

At many profit levels the company owner pays **more tax** than the sole trader. For example, a business owner with profits of £150,000 will pay £130 more tax by using a company, with profits of £250,000 he will pay £1,639 more tax and with profits of £500,000 he will pay £8,792 more tax.

At some profit levels (for example, between £50,000 and £140,000) the company owner pays less tax than the sole trader but not much less and some or all of these savings would be eaten up by higher accountancy fees.

Before the dividend tax increase in April 2016 the company owner would have paid much less tax than the sole trader.

This does NOT mean that business owners should no longer use companies. As we shall discover in the chapters that follow there are lots of circumstances in which a company can be used to save tax.

TABLE 3
Company vs Sole Trader: All Profits Taken as Dividends

Profits	Company Tax	Sole Trader Tax	Saving
10,000	£1,900	£313	-£1,587
20,000	£3,800	£2,913	-£887
30,000	£6,285	£5,813	-£472
40,000	£8,793	£8,713	-£79
50,000	£11,300	£12,263	£963
60,000	£14,708	£16,463	£1,756
70,000	£19,240	£20,663	£1,423
80,000	£23,773	£24,863	£1,091
90,000	£28,305	£29,063	£758
100,000	£32,838	£33,263	£426
110,000	£37,370	£39,463	£2,093
120,000	£41,903	£45,663	£3,761
130,000	£47,296	£50,463	£3,167
140,000	£53,145	£54,663	£1,518
150,000	£58,994	£58,863	-£130
160,000	£63,770	£63,563	-£207
170,000	£68,303	£68,263	-£39
180,000	£72,835	£72,963	£128
190,000	£77,586	£77,663	£78
200,000	£82,572	£82,363	-£209
225,000	£95,037	£94,113	-£924
250,000	£107,503	£105,863	-£1,639
275,000	£119,968	£117,613	-£2,354
300,000	£132,433	£129,363	-£3,070
350,000	£157,364	£152,863	-£4,500
400,000	£182,294	£176,363	-£5,931
450,000	£207,225	£199,863	-£7,361
500,000	£232,155	£223,363	-£8,792
600,000	£282,016	£270,363	-£11,653
700,000	£331,877	£317,363	-£14,514
800,000	£381,738	£364,363	-£17,375
900,000	£431,599	£411,363	-£20,236
1,000,000	£481,460	£458,363	-£23,097

Scottish Company Owners

As stated in the previous chapter, the Scottish Parliament can now set the income tax rates and thresholds for most types of income except dividends and interest.

Thus a Scottish company owner who takes all of his income as dividends will be subject to the tax rates and thresholds applying in the rest of the UK and not the Scottish ones.

In other words, the amounts of tax illustrated in Table 3 apply equally to Scottish company owners. By contrast, sole traders in Scotland who earn more than £45,000 will pay £400 more income tax.

Chapter 11

Company Owners: Tax-free Salaries

In this chapter we'll show how company owners can increase their tax savings by paying themselves a small salary as well as dividends.

We'll assume the company owner has no other income. This keeps the number crunching simple.

Why a Small Salary Is Usually Tax Efficient

The first few thousand pounds of either salary or dividends are tax-free in the hands of the company owner, if the payments fall below the various income tax and national insurance thresholds.

However, a dividend payment is not necessarily tax efficient for the company (and, of course, most company owners are equally concerned about their company's tax position as their own personal tax position).

Dividends are paid out of a company's *after-tax profits*, i.e., after corporation tax has been paid. So every dividend has a corporation tax bill attached to it.

A salary, on the other hand, is a tax deductible expense for the company. Salaries are subject to national insurance (both for the director and the company) but salaries below £8,164 have no national insurance consequences.

In summary, a small salary is more tax efficient than a dividend. Not only is it tax free in the hands of the company owner, it provides a corporation tax saving for the company as well.

This corporation tax saving is essentially a cashback for the company and is why the company owner should consider taking a salary, even if the money isn't needed.

How Much Salary?

There are two important income tax and national insurance thresholds for the 2017/18 tax year:

- National insurance   £8,164
- Income tax   £11,500

Where the company already uses up its £3,000 national insurance employment allowance paying salaries to other employees the "optimal" salary for many company owners is £8,164.

A salary of £8,164 will not attract any employee's or employer's national insurance and, providing the company owner has no other income, will also be free from income tax.

This is also the optimal salary for directors of "one man band" companies which aren't entitled to any employment allowance (see Chapter 9).

Because salaries are usually a tax deductible expense, a salary of £8,164 will save the company £1,551 in corporation tax:

$$£8,164 \times 19\% \text{ corporation tax} = £1,551$$

In other words, it will cost the company just £6,613 to put £8,164 of tax-free cash in the hands of the director.

I placed the word "optimal" in inverted commas because every company and company owner is different. Clearly, a salary of £8,164 will not be optimal for every single company owner in the land. There are many other factors that may influence your salary decision.

Why not take a salary of £11,500 instead of £8,164 to use up your income tax personal allowance? This will be less tax efficient, one reason being that the extra salary will attract both employee's and employer's national insurance, at 12% and 13.8% respectively.

However, the extra tax cost is not significant. Basic-rate taxpayers will typically be around £160 worse off by taking a salary of £11,500 instead of £8,164 and many higher-rate taxpayers will typically be around £225 worse off.

A salary of £11,500 may be preferable when the company does not use up all of its £3,000 national insurance employment allowance paying salaries to other employees. This is because the higher salary will be exempt from employer's national insurance.

In these circumstances basic-rate taxpayers could save around £185 by taking a salary of £11,500 instead of £8,164 and higher-rate taxpayers could save around £27.

Having said this, a lower salary may still be preferable. For example, if the company doesn't have any other employees, the directors may decide to pay themselves a salary of £8,164 each to avoid the hassle of having to make any national insurance payments (for example, to avoid late payment penalties).

Although a salary of £8,164 is completely tax free, it still has to be reported to HMRC as part of the normal payroll process (although it may be possible to make a single annual payroll submission in some circumstances).

Higher Salaries

Although the salaries discussed in this chapter are "optimal" from a strict comparison of tax rates and thresholds, there may be other tax and non-tax reasons why you may wish to pay yourself a higher salary.

Summary

Whether you take a salary of £8,164, £11,500, or something in between, probably won't make a huge amount of difference to many company owners at the end of the day.

Some company owners may wish to pay themselves a salary of £11,500 because, although strictly speaking not "optimal", this lets them take a bigger chunk of income out of the company on a regular basis, without some of the hassle that comes with paying dividends (for example, making sure the company has sufficient distributable profits and that dividends are properly declared).

In all the examples that follow in which we compare the tax paid by self-employed business owners and company owners, we will assume, for better or worse, that the company owner takes a salary of £8,164 and the rest of his income as dividends.

Although a higher or lower salary may be "optimal" or desirable, the additional savings are usually quite small. In other words, using £8,164 is probably perfectly adequate when it comes to examining the tax savings that can be achieved by using a company.

Scottish Company Owners

Any Scottish company owner who takes a small tax-free salary and his remaining income as dividends will pay exactly the same amount of tax as a company owner living elsewhere in the UK.

This is because, although the Scottish Parliament can set the tax rates and thresholds for most types of income, it does not have any power over:

- The income tax personal allowance
- National insurance rates and thresholds
- Dividend taxation
- Corporation tax

Thus in all the examples in which we compare the tax bills of company owners and self-employed business owners in the chapters that follow, the tax bills for company owners are equally relevant to Scottish company owners.

By contrast, the tax bills for self-employed business owners are too low. Self-employed business owners in Scotland who earn more than £45,000 this year will pay £400 more income tax than self-employed business owners in the rest of the UK.

For Scottish business owners one of the benefits of using a company is they can completely shelter themselves from higher income tax in Scotland. Sole traders and partnerships, on the other hand, are fully exposed to "tartan taxes".

Chapter 12

Salaries: Pension Benefits

Apart from being tax efficient a salary confers two extra benefits on company owners:

- State pension entitlement
- Ability to make private pension contributions

State Pension Entitlement

To protect your state pension entitlement you should pay yourself a salary that is greater than the national insurance 'lower earnings limit'.

For 2017/18, the lower earnings limit is £113 per week which requires a total annual salary of at least £5,876.

If you want to protect your state pension entitlement, a salary of at least £5,876 should be paid in 2017/18 in preference to taking dividends.

Private Pension Contributions

Everyone under the age of 75 can make a pension contribution of £3,600 per year. The actual cash contribution would be £2,880, with the taxman adding £720 to bring the total gross contribution to £3,600.

If you want to make bigger pension contributions the contributions you make personally (as opposed to contributions made by your company) must not exceed your 'relevant UK earnings'. Salaries count as earnings, dividends do not.

For a company director taking the "optimal" tax-free salary of £8,164, the maximum pension contribution he can make is £8,164.

This is the maximum *gross* contribution. The director would personally invest £6,531 (£8,164 x 0.8) and the taxman will top this up with £1,633 of basic-rate tax relief for a gross contribution of £8,164.

Similarly, a director taking a salary of £11,500 can make a maximum pension contribution of £11,500. The director would personally invest £9,200 (£11,500 x 0.8) and the taxman will top this up with £2,300 of basic-rate tax relief for a gross contribution of £11,500.

Directors who want to make bigger pension contributions have two choices:

- Pay themselves a bigger salary (i.e. more earnings)
- Get the company to make the pension contributions

Company pension contributions are certainly very tax efficient, as they generally provide corporation tax relief for the company and also avoid national insurance.

It is possible that HMRC will deny the company tax relief if the pension contribution, together with the director's other remuneration, amounts to more than a commercial rate of pay for the job they do for the company.

This problem is fairly rare in practice but could affect any company owner who does not play a fully active role in the day-to-day management of their business.

Chapter 13

Company vs Sole Trader: Tax-Free Salary & Dividends

In this chapter we'll compare the total tax paid by sole traders and company owners when the company owner pays himself a salary of £8,164 and extracts the remaining profits as dividends.

Table 4 compares the total tax (corporation tax and income tax) payable by a company owner with the total tax (income tax and national insurance) payable by a sole trader.

Comparing Table 4 with Table 3 (all profits taken as dividends) we can see that a salary of £8,164 reduces the company owner's overall tax bill by at least £1,000 at many profit levels.

However, as profits increase the benefit of taking a salary diminishes and when profits are £190,000 or more the company owner's tax bill actually *increases* slightly by taking a salary. As pointed out earlier, there are other reasons why a salary may be desirable, for example to protect your state pension entitlement.

Table 4 also reveals that company owners with profits between £20,000 and £140,000 pay less tax overall than sole traders. However, the savings are not huge (typically between around £2,000 and £3,000). A sizeable chunk of those savings could be gobbled up by higher accountancy fees.

The savings were far higher before the dividend tax rates were increased on 6 April 2016.

Table 4 also reveals that, when profits exceed £150,000, company owners currently pay more tax than sole traders when all profits are extracted. For example, a company owner with profits of £300,000 will pay £3,130 more tax than a sole trader.

One would normally associate big profits with companies and small profits with sole traders but what Table 4 reveals is that those businesses that make the most profit are currently better off being taxed as sole traders!

TABLE 4
Company vs Sole Trader: £8,164 Salary & Dividends

Profits	Company Tax	Sole Trader Tax	Saving
10,000	£349	£313	-£35
20,000	£2,343	£2,913	£571
30,000	£4,850	£5,813	£963
40,000	£7,358	£8,713	£1,356
50,000	£9,865	£12,263	£2,398
60,000	£13,661	£16,463	£2,802
70,000	£18,193	£20,663	£2,470
80,000	£22,725	£24,863	£2,138
90,000	£27,258	£29,063	£1,805
100,000	£31,790	£33,263	£1,473
110,000	£36,323	£39,463	£3,140
120,000	£40,855	£45,663	£4,808
130,000	£46,512	£50,463	£3,951
140,000	£52,867	£54,663	£1,796
150,000	£59,211	£58,863	-£348
160,000	£63,743	£63,563	-£180
170,000	£68,276	£68,263	-£13
180,000	£72,808	£72,963	£155
190,000	£77,646	£77,663	£17
200,000	£82,633	£82,363	-£270
225,000	£95,098	£94,113	-£984
250,000	£107,563	£105,863	-£1,699
275,000	£120,028	£117,613	-£2,415
300,000	£132,493	£129,363	-£3,130
350,000	£157,424	£152,863	-£4,560
400,000	£182,354	£176,363	-£5,991
450,000	£207,285	£199,863	-£7,421
500,000	£232,215	£223,363	-£8,852
600,000	£282,076	£270,363	-£11,713
700,000	£331,937	£317,363	-£14,574
800,000	£381,798	£364,363	-£17,435
900,000	£431,659	£411,363	-£20,296
1,000,000	£481,520	£458,363	-£23,157

How the Tax Bills Are Calculated

Taking a sample profit figure from Table 4 – £60,000 – let's examine how the numbers are calculated:

Sole Trader Tax Calculation

Income tax:	£
Profits	60,000
Less: Personal allowance	11,500
Taxable profits	48,500
£33,500 @ 20%	6,700
£15,000 @ 40%	6,000
Total	12,700

National insurance:	
Class 2 (£2.85 per week)	148
Class 4:	
£45,000 - £8,164 @ 9%	3,315
£60,000 - £45,000 @ 2%	300
Total	3,763

Total income tax and national insurance: £16,463

Company Tax Calculation

Corporation tax:	£
Profits	60,000
Less: salary	8,164
Taxable profits	51,836
Corporation tax @ 19%	9,849
After-tax profits/dividend	41,987

Income tax on dividend:	
Remaining tax-free personal allowance:	
(£11,500 - £8,164)	3,336
Tax-free dividend allowance	5,000
Basic-rate band (£33,500-£5,000)	28,500
Basic-rate tax @ 7.5%	2,138
Taxed at higher rate	5,151
Higher-rate tax @ 32.5%	1,674
Total income tax	3,812

Total corporation tax and income tax: £13,661

Let's take another profit figure from Table 4 – £200,000 – and examine a slightly more complicated calculation:

Sole Trader Tax Calculation

Income tax:	£
Profits	200,000
Less: Personal allowance	0
Taxable profits	200,000
£33,500 @ 20%	6,700
£116,500 @ 40%	46,600
£50,000 @ 45%	22,500
Total	75,800

National insurance:	
Class 2 (£2.85 per week)	148
Class 4:	
£45,000 - £8,164 @ 9%	3,315
£200,000 - £45,000 @ 2%	3,100
Total	6,563

Total income tax and national insurance: £82,363

Company Tax Calculation

Corporation tax:	£
Profits	200,000
Less: salary	8,164
Taxable profits	191,836
Corporation tax @ 19%	36,449
After-tax profits/dividend	155,387

Income tax	
Income tax on salary (£8,164 x 20%)	1,633
Tax-free dividend allowance	5,000
Basic-rate band (£33,500-£8,164-£5,000)	20,336
Basic-rate tax @ 7.5%	1,525
Higher-rate band	116,500
Higher-rate tax @ 32.5%	37,863
Taxed at additional rate	13,551
Additional rate tax @ 38.1%	5,163
Total income tax	46,184

Total corporation tax and income tax: £82,633

Scottish Taxpayers

The "company tax" numbers in Table 4 apply equally to Scottish company owners. The "sole trader tax" numbers are too low. Sole traders who earn more than £45,000 will pay £400 more income tax in Scotland this year, which makes using a company relatively more attractive.

Should I Use a Company?

I doubt many individuals who currently run a sole trader business will rush out and set up a company based solely on the potential tax savings illustrated in Table 4.

Even where profits are at a level that produces a potential tax saving, the saving may not be big enough to compensate for the hassle and expense of converting an existing unincorporated business into a company, or to cover the higher ongoing costs of running a company.

Having said this, it's important to point out that Table 4, though interesting, does not include all of the tax benefits and drawbacks of using a company. In Part 7 we move beyond a strict comparison of tax rates and look at some of the other tax benefits and drawbacks of being a company owner or sole trader.

There are two other important reasons why using company could still produce attractive tax savings:

- More money can be kept in the business
- Corporation tax will be cut further

So far, in all of the comparisons of company owners and sole traders, we have assumed that the company owner extracts all the profits from the business. However, many company owners keep some profits in the company for two reasons:

- To avoid extortionate income tax rates
- To reinvest and grow the business

This is where companies really show their mettle and can produce significant tax savings.

In Part 6 we will see how company owners can alter the amount of income they extract and avoid various income thresholds where extortionate tax rates apply (sole traders cannot do this).

In the next chapter we take a look at how company owners who reinvest some of their profits often have a lot more financial firepower than sole traders.

Corporation Tax Cuts

The corporation tax rate was reduced from 20% to 19% on 1 April 2017. The rate will be reduced again from 19% to 17% from 1 April 2020.

In Northern Ireland the rate is set to be cut to 12.5% in the near future when corporation tax powers are devolved to the Northern Ireland Assembly.

The recent cut from 20% to 19% probably hasn't made much difference to most business owners' incorporation decision. Companies now get to keep 1% more of their profits and company owners will receive slightly less after paying income tax.

Take a company which is left with a profit of £100,000 after paying the company owner's own salary. The cut in corporation tax from 20% to 19% will leave the company with £1,000 more after-tax profit to distribute as a dividend. After paying tax at 32.5% the company owner will be left with £675 more income.

Thus, the corporation tax cut will result in the company owner's income increasing by an amount equal to 0.675% of the company's pre-tax profit.

If the company owner is a basic-rate taxpayer, paying 7.5% tax on his dividend income, the corporation tax cut will result in his income increasing by an amount equal to 0.925% of the company's pre-tax profit.

Potential Tax Savings in 2020/21

Let's move forward to the 2020/21 tax year when the corporation tax rate will fall to 17%.

Table 5 compares the total tax (corporation tax and income tax) payable by a company owner with the total tax (income tax and national insurance) payable by a sole trader. Once again it is assumed that the company owner extracts all the profits.

Clearly, at most profit levels using a company will be more attractive than it is at present. For example, at present a business owner with profits of £100,000 can save £1,473 tax by using a company. By the time we get to 2020/21 that tax saving could increase to £2,829.

A business owner with profits of £250,000 currently pays £1,699 more tax by using a company. When we get to 2020/21 the position reverses and a company could produce a saving of £1,407.

The potential savings do, however, vary considerably at different profit levels and company owners will still pay more tax than sole traders when profits exceed £350,000.

Table 5 Assumptions

The numbers in Table 5 are calculated by making the following assumptions:

- Corporation tax is reduced to 17%
- The income tax higher-rate threshold is £50,000
- The personal allowance is £12,500
- The dividend allowance is £2,000
- Class 2 national insurance is abolished
- The national insurance threshold is £8,750

The Government has committed to raising the personal allowance to £12,500 by 2020/21 and the higher-rate threshold to £50,000.

Class 2 national insurance will be abolished from April 2018.

The national insurance threshold increases each year in line with inflation, so the number £8,750 is simply an estimate.

TABLE 5
Company vs Sole Trader: 2020/21 Estimated

Profits	Company Tax	Sole Trader Tax	Saving
10,000	£213	£113	-£100
20,000	£2,182	£2,513	£331
30,000	£4,504	£5,413	£908
40,000	£6,827	£8,313	£1,486
50,000	£9,149	£11,213	£2,063
60,000	£11,793	£15,413	£3,619
70,000	£16,191	£19,613	£3,422
80,000	£20,588	£23,813	£3,224
90,000	£24,986	£28,013	£3,027
100,000	£29,383	£32,213	£2,829
110,000	£33,781	£38,413	£4,632
120,000	£38,355	£44,613	£6,257
130,000	£44,219	£49,813	£5,593
140,000	£50,484	£54,013	£3,528
150,000	£56,527	£58,213	£1,685
160,000	£60,925	£62,913	£1,988
170,000	£65,322	£67,613	£2,290
180,000	£69,769	£72,313	£2,543
190,000	£74,632	£77,013	£2,381
200,000	£79,494	£81,713	£2,219
225,000	£91,650	£93,463	£1,813
250,000	£103,805	£105,213	£1,407
275,000	£115,961	£116,963	£1,001
300,000	£128,117	£128,713	£596
350,000	£152,428	£152,213	-£216
400,000	£176,740	£175,713	-£1,027
450,000	£201,051	£199,213	-£1,839
500,000	£225,363	£222,713	-£2,650
600,000	£273,986	£269,713	-£4,273
700,000	£322,609	£316,713	-£5,896
800,000	£371,232	£363,713	-£7,519
900,000	£419,855	£410,713	-£9,142
1,000,000	£468,478	£457,713	-£10,765

Other than these changes it's assumed that all tax rates remain the same. Of course, this is arguably a foolhardy assumption because the Government is constantly fiddling with the tax system!

For example, if dividend tax rates are increased again using a company could become unattractive, despite the cuts in corporation tax. Conversely, if the national insurance paid by sole traders is increased, this could make using a company more attractive.

And this brings us neatly to the most important point about using a company to save tax: any potential tax saving that you may enjoy could be taken away at the drop of a hat by the Government.

Scottish Taxpayers

The "company tax" tax bills in Table 5 apply equally to Scottish company owners.

The "sole trader tax" tax bills are probably too low for Scottish taxpayers who will probably start paying 40% tax when their income is less than £50,000.

In other words, Scottish business owners will probably enjoy bigger tax savings by using a company than business owners in the rest of the UK.

Chapter 14

Reinvesting Profits to Make Bigger Tax Savings

Company owners have a lot more flexibility than sole traders: The profits of the business can either be kept inside the company or extracted as income.

This is one of the key tax benefits of using a company. Only corporation tax is payable on profits that are retained in the company. The company owners do not have to pay any additional income tax.

By contrast, sole traders pay income tax and national insurance on ALL their profits, irrespective of whether they are retained within the business or taken out as drawings.

Table 6 compares the total tax (corporation tax and income tax) payable by a company owner with the total tax (income tax and national insurance) payable by a sole trader. Again we assume that the company owner takes a salary of £8,164 and takes the rest of his income as dividends.

The difference between this table and Table 4 from the previous chapter is that the company owner only extracts 50% of the after-tax profits by way of dividend. The remaining profits are kept inside the company to fund future growth of the business.

The total tax bills shown in Table 6 speak for themselves: when a business is growing and using retained earnings as a source of finance, using a company can produce big tax savings.

For example, a business owner with profits of £60,000 could save £5,665 in tax by using a company, a business owner with profits of £80,000 could save £9,658 in tax and a business owner with profits of £120,000 could save £19,528 in tax.

Remember these are *annual savings* – it may be possible to enjoy similar savings every year.

TABLE 6
Company vs Sole Trader: 50% Profits Reinvested

Profits	Company Tax	Sole Trader Tax	Saving
10,000	£349	£313	-£35
20,000	£2,249	£2,913	£665
30,000	£4,187	£5,813	£1,627
40,000	£6,391	£8,713	£2,323
50,000	£8,594	£12,263	£3,669
60,000	£10,798	£16,463	£5,665
70,000	£13,002	£20,663	£7,662
80,000	£15,206	£24,863	£9,658
90,000	£17,409	£29,063	£11,654
100,000	£19,703	£33,263	£13,561
110,000	£22,919	£39,463	£16,545
120,000	£26,135	£45,663	£19,528
130,000	£29,351	£50,463	£21,112
140,000	£32,568	£54,663	£22,096
150,000	£35,784	£58,863	£23,080
160,000	£39,000	£63,563	£24,563
170,000	£42,216	£68,263	£26,047
180,000	£45,433	£72,963	£27,531
190,000	£48,649	£77,663	£29,015
200,000	£51,865	£82,363	£30,498
225,000	£59,906	£94,113	£34,208
250,000	£68,939	£105,863	£36,925
275,000	£79,222	£117,613	£38,391
300,000	£88,786	£129,363	£40,578
350,000	£104,867	£152,863	£47,997
400,000	£121,892	£176,363	£54,471
450,000	£139,107	£199,863	£60,756
500,000	£156,323	£223,363	£67,041
600,000	£190,753	£270,363	£79,610
700,000	£225,184	£317,363	£92,180
800,000	£259,614	£364,363	£104,749
900,000	£294,045	£411,363	£117,319
1,000,000	£328,475	£458,363	£129,888

How the Tax Bills Are Calculated

Taking a sample profit figure from Table 6 – £100,000 – let's examine how the company tax numbers are calculated (the sole trader figures are the same as in Table 4):

Company Tax Calculation

Corporation tax:	£
Profits	100,000
Less: salary	8,164
Taxable profits	91,836
Corporation tax @ 19%	17,449
After-tax profits	74,387
Dividend (50%)	37,194

Income tax on dividend:	
Remaining tax-free personal allowance:	
(£11,500 - £8,164)	3,336
Tax-free dividend allowance	5,000
Basic-rate band (£33,500-£5,000)	28,500
Basic-rate tax @ 7.5%	2,138
Taxed at higher rate	358
Higher-rate tax @ 32.5%	116
Total income tax	2,254

Total corporation tax and income tax: £19,703

A sole trader who makes identical profits will pay £33,263 in tax.

Why are the tax savings so large for the company owner? Despite making a profit of £100,000, the company owner doesn't pay much income tax because a lot of the profit is left inside the company.

With a salary of £8,164 and dividend of just £37,194 the company owner's total taxable income is £45,358. His salary and £8,336 of his dividend income is tax free. He has to pay 7.5% tax on a big chunk of his dividend income but just £358 is taxed at the 32.5% higher rate.

In contrast, the sole trader pays 40% income tax on a big chunk of his profit (£55,000).

Sole Traders Can Reinvest Profits Too!

It's important to point out that sole traders can also reduce their tax bills and grow their businesses by reinvesting profits.

For example, the annual investment allowance lets businesses claim an immediate 100% tax deduction when they buy equipment and machinery for their businesses. Since January 2016 the allowance has been fixed permanently at £200,000 per year.

There are lots of other items on which sole traders can claim tax relief. See the Taxcafe guide *Small Business Tax Saving Tactics* for full details.

For example, if a sole trader increases his tax deductible spending by £1,000 before the end of his tax year he will reduce his taxable profits by £1,000 and save £420 in income tax and national insurance if he is a higher-rate taxpayer.

Similarly, companies can reinvest their profits before corporation tax becomes payable. If a company increases its tax deductible spending by £1,000 before the end of its accounting period it will reduce its taxable profits by £1,000 and save £190 in corporation tax. Thus it's far better, where possible, to reinvest profits before the end of the accounting period to save not just income tax but corporation tax as well.

However, the sole trader may face a bigger timing problem than the company owner. Any profits that the sole trader fails to reinvest before the end of his tax year will be subject to income tax and national insurance in full.

By contrast, if a company fails to reinvest its profits before the end of its accounting period the only tax payable will be corporation tax because income tax is only payable when profits are extracted.

Finally, it's also worth pointing out that sole traders don't have to reinvest in their businesses to reduce their tax bills – they can also make pension contributions.

Similarly, a company owner can get the company to make pension contributions which will reduce its corporation tax bill.

See the Taxcafe guide *Pension Magic* for full details.

Danger of Holding Too Much Cash?

One reason why you should consider extracting cash from your company, even if this results in an income tax bill, is to reduce exposure to business risk.

Furthermore, if your company holds too many non-trading assets, including surplus cash, this may prejudice its status as a trading company. This means that you may not be able to, for example, claim Entrepreneurs Relief when the company is sold or wound up.

Cash may be treated as 'surplus' if you cannot show that it will be required by the business in the future. It may therefore be helpful to draw up a business plan showing how any cash balance will be used by the business.

However, provided the cash has been generated from trading activities and is not actively managed as an investment, holding large cash balances should not be considered a non-trading activity.

Potential Tax Savings in 2020/21

Let's move forward to the 2020/21 tax year when the corporation tax rate is expected to fall to 17%.

Table 7 compares the total tax (corporation tax and income tax) payable by a company owner with the total tax (income tax and national insurance) payable by a sole trader.

The 2020/21 tax bills are calculated in the same way as those in Table 5 except the company owner only extracts 50% of the after-tax profits by way of a dividend. The remaining profits are kept inside the company to fund future growth of the business.

Once again we can see that using a company is most powerful when profits are reinvested and the savings may be even greater at most profit levels when the corporation tax rate is reduced to 17%.

TABLE 7
50% Profits Reinvested: 2020/21 Estimated

Profits	Company Tax	Sole Trader Tax	Saving
10,000	£213	£113	-£100
20,000	£1,913	£2,513	£600
30,000	£3,843	£5,413	£1,570
40,000	£5,854	£8,313	£2,459
50,000	£7,865	£11,213	£3,347
60,000	£9,876	£15,413	£5,536
70,000	£11,888	£19,613	£7,725
80,000	£13,899	£23,813	£9,914
90,000	£15,910	£28,013	£12,102
100,000	£17,921	£32,213	£14,291
110,000	£20,125	£38,413	£18,288
120,000	£23,174	£44,613	£21,439
130,000	£26,222	£49,813	£23,590
140,000	£29,271	£54,013	£24,741
150,000	£32,320	£58,213	£25,893
160,000	£35,369	£62,913	£27,544
170,000	£38,417	£67,613	£29,195
180,000	£41,466	£72,313	£30,846
190,000	£44,515	£77,013	£32,498
200,000	£47,564	£81,713	£34,149
225,000	£55,185	£93,463	£38,277
250,000	£64,334	£105,213	£40,878
275,000	£74,290	£116,963	£42,672
300,000	£83,207	£128,713	£45,505
350,000	£98,472	£152,213	£53,741
400,000	£114,877	£175,713	£60,835
450,000	£131,283	£199,213	£67,929
500,000	£147,689	£222,713	£75,024
600,000	£180,500	£269,713	£89,212
700,000	£213,312	£316,713	£103,401
800,000	£246,123	£363,713	£117,589
900,000	£278,935	£410,713	£131,778
1,000,000	£311,746	£457,713	£145,966

Part 4

Salaries & Dividends: Practical Issues & Dangers

Chapter 15

How to Avoid the Minimum Wage Rules

If you take a small salary from your company (for example, £8,164 or £11,500) there is a danger of falling foul of the national minimum wage (NMW) or the new national living wage (NLW).

Where wages are too low, HMRC will force the company to make up the shortfall. Bigger wage payments may result in bigger national insurance bills for both the company and the director.

There is also a penalty equivalent to 200% of the unpaid wages with a maximum penalty of £20,000 per worker. Those found guilty will also be considered for disqualification from being a company director for up to 15 years.

However, the key point to note about the NMW/NLW is that it only applies to directors who have a contract of employment.

Due to the informal set up in many small companies, there may be some uncertainty as to whether an employment contract exists between the director and the company (employment contracts do not need to be in writing).

However, it is generally accepted amongst the tax profession that if you do not issue yourself with an explicit contract of employment the minimum wage regulations will not apply.

This means you should be able to continue paying yourself a small salary, even if it is less than the national minimum wage or national living wage.

However, risk averse company owners (those worried about potential penalties) should consider paying themselves enough salary to satisfy the minimum wage regulations.

National Living Wage Rates

The new national living wage applies to those aged 25 and over. The rate is currently £7.50 per hour.

If you spend, say, 35 hours per week actively managing your business, the total salary due for 2017/18 will be:

35 x 52 weeks x £7.50 = £13,650

Fortunately this is not hugely higher than the optimal salary amounts but will still result in unwelcome national insurance charges.

The national insurance payable on this salary by the director would be £658 and £757 would be payable by the company (£0 if the company has spare employment allowance).

Of course, every case is different and some directors will be able to argue that they spend fewer hours actively managing the business.

Although it may seem that the best strategy is to simply not have a contract of employment, there may be other reasons why having such a contract is important.

Company Owners Who Aren't Directors

It is possible that some family members will be employees of the company but not directors. These individuals are subject to the NMW or NLW for all hours spent working in the business (although directors are exempt with respect to hours spent performing their duties as directors).

However, it is possible that if they only work part time, the salary that must be paid to them will still be within the optimal amounts of £8,164 or £11,500.

Chapter 16

Is My Salary Tax Deductible?

One of the benefits of getting your company to pay you a salary is that the amount will normally be a tax deductible expense and reduce the company's corporation tax bill.

However, it is important to point out that there is no automatic right to corporation tax relief. The amount paid has to be justified by the work carried out for the business and the individual's level of responsibility.

While this may not be an important issue for company owners who work full time in the business and pay themselves a small salary, it may be important if you start paying salaries to other family members, in particular those who only work on a part time basis.

The question of whether your employment income will attract corporation tax relief may also become an issue if you decide to pay yourself a large one-off bonus.

Some of the factors that may determine whether a salary or bonus payment is tax deductible include:

- The number of hours worked in the business

- The individual's legal obligations and responsibilities (e.g. directors' duties)

- The amount of pay received by the company's other employees

- The pay received by employees at other companies performing similar roles

- The company's performance and ability to pay salaries/bonuses.

In the case of large one-off bonus payments made only to the company's directors/shareholders it may be necessary to document the commercial rationale for the payment to show that the payment is justifiable. This can be done in the minutes of a directors' board meeting.

It may also be advisable to record the approval of any bonus in the minutes of a shareholders' meeting.

Chapter 17

Paying Salaries & Dividends: Profits & Paperwork

Salaries – Real Time Information

Since April 2013 employers have had to report salary payments to HMRC under the Real Time Information (RTI) regime. Under real time information, employers are required to submit a Full Payment Submission (FPS) to HMRC at the same time or before each payment is made to a director or employee.

The idea is to make sure the right amount of tax is paid at the right time. Under the previous system, employers generally only had to report payroll information to HMRC at the end of the year.

Under RTI the directors own salaries could result in additional payroll costs (for example, in small husband and wife companies or 'one man band' companies, where the only salaries paid are those of the directors themselves).

Where the directors receive small salaries, it may be cheaper and easier to register with HMRC as an annual scheme and pay salaries as a single annual lump sum (e.g. in March just before the end of the tax year).

With annual schemes an FPS is only expected in the month of payment and HMRC only has to be paid once a year. However, it is only possible to register as an annual scheme if all employees are paid annually at the same time.

Once a business is registered as an annual scheme, an Employer Payment Summary (EPS) is not required for the 11 months of the tax year where no payments are made to the directors. Schemes not registered as annual schemes have to make monthly submissions, even if no salaries are paid.

An additional problem may arise where directors withdraw cash from their companies and only later decide how these payments are to be treated (for example, as salaries or dividends).

Where the director's loan account is overdrawn, an amount withdrawn and subsequently designated as salary could result in a late filing penalty under RTI.

When directors withdraw money from their companies it is essential to decide up front the nature of the payment (e.g. salary, loan, dividend, reimbursement of expenses) and to have evidence supporting that decision.

For example, where a director borrows money from the company, the terms of the loan should be set out in writing. Withdrawals by directors that cannot be categorised might be treated as earnings by HMRC unless the company can prove otherwise.

Dividends

Distributable Profits

Under the Companies Act a company cannot legally pay a dividend unless it has sufficient distributable profits to cover it.

A company's distributable profits are its accumulated realised profits, less accumulated realised losses. This information can generally be found in the company's most recent annual accounts.

It is not necessary for the company to actually make a profit in the year the dividend is paid, as long as there are sufficient accumulated profits (after tax) from previous years.

If the distributable profits are not big enough to cover the dividend it may be necessary to prepare interim management accounts to justify the payment. A revaluation of an investment property is not a realised profit.

Before paying any dividends it is probably wise to speak to your accountant to check whether the company does indeed have sufficient distributable profits.

It may also be wise to check whether a loss has been realised since the last accounts were drawn up and whether any dividend will cause cash flow problems for the company.

In general, it is wise to be conservative and keep dividends to a reasonable level.

If the company does not have sufficient distributable profits to cover its dividend payments, the dividends will be illegal and the shareholder will be liable to repay the company. If not repaid it could be treated as a loan, resulting in a 32.5% section 455 charge.

Dividend Formalities & Paperwork

It is possible that HMRC will try to tax dividends as employment income. To help avoid any such challenge it is essential to ensure that dividends are properly declared and you have the supporting paperwork to prove it.

This includes:

- Holding a directors' board meeting to recommend the dividend payment (with printed minutes to prove the meeting took place)

- Holding a general meeting of the company's members (i.e. shareholders) to approve the dividend payment (with printed minutes to prove the meeting took place).

- Issuing a dividend voucher to each shareholder.

Some commentators also argue that it is not advisable to declare dividends monthly because this will look more like salary income, especially if the above formalities are neglected.

A better alternative would be an infrequent dividend credited to the director's loan account which can then be drawn down throughout the year.

Paying a dividend towards the end of the tax year, when it may be easier to work out how much income tax will be payable, is possibly best in timing terms. If a dividend is paid at the beginning of the year and income from other sources (e.g. rental income) turns out to be higher than expected, the company owner could end up paying tax at a higher rate on his dividend income.

Chapter 18

Dividends Taxed as Earnings

Recent tax cases demonstrate the potential danger that dividends paid to a director/shareholder may in some circumstances be vulnerable to a national insurance liability and possibly a full PAYE charge.

It remains to be seen how HMRC will choose to use these decisions in the context of family companies:

P A Holdings

PA Holdings switched from a conventional bonus arrangement to a more intricate structure whereby an employee benefit trust was funded by the company, which in turn awarded preference shares to employees. These preference shares duly paid a dividend after which they were redeemed.

The company and its employees argued that the dividends should be taxed as dividends using dividend tax rates and without any PAYE or national insurance implications.

By contrast, HMRC took the view that the dividends simply amounted to earnings and that the normal PAYE and national insurance payments should have been deducted from them and accounted for to HMRC.

The Court of Appeal overturned the decisions of the First Tier Tribunal and the Upper Tribunal and decided that the dividends were indeed earnings for employment and should therefore suffer deductions of income tax at source through PAYE. Both employers and employees national insurance deductions should also have been made.

PA Holdings initially decided to appeal to the Supreme Court but later threw in the towel. This led to fears that HMRC could attack director/shareholders who take most of their income as dividends.

Many tax advisers argue that the aggressive tax planning undertaken by PA Holdings (trying to change bonuses into dividends for a large chunk of employees) is entirely different to the profit extraction model of most small companies.

In other words, most director/shareholders should be able to continue paying themselves small salaries and taking the rest of their income as dividends with limited risk of challenge from HMRC.

Uniplex (UK) Ltd

Uniplex was sold a scheme aimed at giving employees dividend income instead of remuneration, issuing different classes of share to each employee. This type of arrangement is generally known as alphabet shares.

The scheme failed as it was not implemented as planned. However, the First Tier Tribunal judge added that the scheme, even if implemented correctly, might still have failed.

Stewart Fraser Ltd

This case involved a write off of loans by a close company to an employee shareholder. The loan write offs were treated as distributions taxable on the employee. HMRC successfully argued that national insurance liabilities were payable by the company on the loan write offs.

Practical Implications

The practical implications relate to the boundary between normal dividend payments and those which under the PA Holdings/Uniplex/Stewart Fraser case principles would be treated as employment earnings and hence attract income tax and national insurance deductions through PAYE. For instance in PA Holdings the First Tier Tribunal said:

"If something is paid out as a distribution by a company to an investing shareholder then the issue of derivation may arise if the shareholder is also an employee. The facts may show that the derivation of a dividend

from a share may not be related to earnings because the acquisition and ownership of the share was not related to earnings or more generally to the status of the individual as an employee of the company".

In Uniplex, the First Tier Tribunal said:

"The PA Holdings case is authority for the proposition that payments from a party other than the employer can be from an employee's employment" and *"It may well have still been the case that the full amount would have been taxable because employees had given no consideration for the payment other than their services".*

Summary

Dividends paid to an employee-shareholder may in some circumstances be vulnerable to a national insurance liability, and possibly to a full PAYE charge. It remains to be seen how HMRC will choose to use these decisions in the context of family companies and remuneration planning generally.

Dividends from certain alphabet share arrangements, that allow profits to be shared in a way that relates to the amount of work carried out in the business, are at risk of being taxed as employment income.

Most at risk are shares that have no capital or voting rights other than a right to dividend income.

Alphabet share arrangements could also fall foul of the settlements legislation if they are used to divert dividend income to another person.

Chapter 19

Small Salary, Big Dividends: Potential Dangers

It is quite common practice for company owners to pay themselves a small salary and take the rest of their income as dividends. Many accountants have been recommending this strategy for years.

However, it is important to point out that some tax advisors are cautious about certain aspects of this tax planning technique, especially in light of court decisions like PA Holdings, where the Court of Appeal decided that certain dividends should be subject to PAYE and national insurance (see Chapter 18).

There is a fear that cases like this will create a wide precedent for any employer that pays dividends to its staff. It is difficult to quantify the potential danger, however, because a lot depends on HMRC's willingness to act. The most vulnerable, arguably, are those that use tax planning techniques that HMRC may view as aggressive, including possibly:

- Large scale contrived arrangements where dividends are created for tax avoidance purposes (as in PA Holdings).

- Directors' loans that are written off and taxed as dividends.

- Dividend waivers that are used to divert income to other shareholders, for example where a director waives his own dividends so that his wife can receive more income. HMRC succeeded in challenging dividend waivers in the case of *Donovan & McLaren v HMRC*.

- Certain 'Alphabet' share arrangements, where different classes of shares (A, B, C etc) have no substantive rights other than to dividends. These arrangements are often used to substitute dividends for bonuses.

- Situations where previous salaries have been reduced in favour of dividends.

The sixty-four thousand dollar question is: where does this leave the average small company owner taking a small salary and the rest of his income as dividends?

At the time of writing it would appear that most small companies are not under attack but this state of affairs could change at any time. The small salary/big dividend tax planning technique does not produce guaranteed tax savings. There is a danger, no matter how small, that HMRC may try to tax your dividends as earnings, if not now then at some point in the future.

Also, with regards to the last point in the above list, please note that some (more conservative) tax advisors argue that if you are currently taking a salary that is larger than the 'optimal' amounts outlined in Chapter 11 you should not reduce it.

Other tax advisors recommend taking a salary slightly larger than the 'optimal' amounts, so that at least some income tax and national insurance is paid by the director.

Finally, remember there is also a danger that dividend tax rates could be increased again at some point in the future. Any increase could completely negate any tax benefit you hope to obtain by running your business as a limited company.

Chapter 20

Personal Service Companies

If your company is classed as a personal service company, many of the tax planning opportunities available to other company owners may not be available, for example, the ability to take dividends that are free from national insurance.

Personal service companies often have to operate the infamous 'IR35' regime which means the company may be forced to calculate a notional salary for the director/shareholder.

This deemed income will be subject to PAYE and national insurance.

Essentially, HMRC may ignore the company set up and treat most of the company's income as employment income.

Which Companies Are Affected by IR35?

This is where it all becomes a bit of a grey area (which is why professional advice is essential!)

A personal service company is, generally speaking, a firm that receives all or most of its income from services provided by the director/shareholder.

Often the work will be carried out for just one client, often for a long period of time, and the client will probably only want the personal services of the company owner (hence IR35 often applies to 'one man band' companies).

Essentially HMRC is looking for cases of 'disguised employment'. In other words, ignoring the fact that there is an intermediary company, the relationship is more like that between an employer and employee rather than the kind of relationship that exists between independent self-employed business owners and their clients.

Where such 'disguised employment' exists, the company must

apply the IR35 regime to the payments received from that client – effectively treating most of those payments as if they were salary paid to the director/shareholder.

A typical situation which might be caught under the IR35 rules is where the individual resigns as an employee and then goes back to the same job but working through a company.

However, it's all very subjective with a long line of legal cases adding to the confusion.

Personal service companies can be found in many different business sectors: the most cited example is IT consultants.

They also came under the media spotlight in recent times when it was disclosed that some BBC presenters had been operating as 'freelancers' via personal service companies, when many would argue that they are in fact nothing but employees of the BBC.

Changes Announced in the March 2016 Budget

In 2015 the Government published a discussion document exploring new ideas, including a proposal that the client engaging the services of a worker providing services through their own limited company should be responsible for deciding whether the IR35 legislation applies and responsible for deducting tax and national insurance.

In the March 2016 Budget it was announced that this approach would be followed by public sector bodies. From April 2017, where a public sector body engages a worker providing services through their own limited company, it will be responsible for determining whether the IR35 rules should apply and for paying the right tax.

There was no mention of a wider application to the private sector use of personal service companies or reform of IR35. However, some tax commentators believe that it is only a matter of time before similar rules are applied to private sector employers.

HMRC's IR35 Digital Tool

HMRC recently launched an online tool to help individuals assess whether the intermediaries legislation applies to any particular engagement:

www.tax.service.gov.uk/check-employment-status-for-tax/setup

It has been widely panned by the experts for being too strict in its assessments.

A key question is "Has the worker's business arranged for someone else (a substitute) to do the work instead of them during this engagement?"

If you don't have the right to send someone as a replacement, it would appear there is little chance of the online tool treating you as outside IR35.

Personal service companies and IR35 are beyond the scope of this guide.

Chapter 21

Future Tax Changes

In this guide we've seen how company owners can end up with lower tax bills than sole traders. However, it is very important to make this point:

The tax savings are not guaranteed or set in stone

The tax regime is constantly changing and it's possible changes will be made that will make it less attractive to use a company – even if those changes only take place several years from now.

Company Owners Taxed as Sole Traders?

In Chapter 4 we pointed out that the Office of Tax Simplification (OTS) looked into a system of "look through" taxation for some small companies.

With lookthrough taxation, instead of paying corporation tax, the company's shareholders would pay income tax and national insurance on all the profits of the business, just like unincorporated businesses (sole traders and partnerships).

By contrast, the advantage of using a company is you can control your income tax bill by paying yourself dividends as and when you like. Sole traders and partnerships must pay income tax and national insurance each year on all the profits of the business.

Furthermore, those who wish to grow their businesses can retain profits inside their companies, in which case the only tax payable is 19% corporation tax (falling to 17% in 2020).

Fortunately, the OTS has decided not to recommend look through taxation because it would not simplify the tax system and harm investment. For now this specific threat has gone away. However, the key point is this:

At the stroke of a pen the Government can take away any tax benefit you hope to achieve by using a company.

Increase in Corporation Tax Rates?

It's unlikely corporation tax will increase in the short term. On the contrary, the Government has been furiously cutting the corporation tax rate in recent years.

The rate was cut from 20% to 19% in April 2017 and will be cut again to 17% in April 2020.

Verdict: an increase in corporation tax is highly unlikely while the current Government is in power.

However, who knows what could happen in the future. Your business, if successful, should outlive many governments and political fashions which means it may eventually be faced with a much less friendly corporate tax environment.

Another Dividend Tax Increase?

In previous editions of this guide I warned that dividends could be taxed more heavily. Now that the tax rates have been increased once, what's to stop them being increased again – for example, what's to stop an increase in the basic rate from 7.5% to 10%?

The General Anti-Abuse Rule

A new general anti-abuse rule (GAAR) came into operation in 2013. Tax arrangements are "abusive" if they cannot reasonably be regarded as a reasonable course of action – this is commonly referred to as the double reasonableness test.

Clearly it's very subjective and HMRC has sought to reassure taxpayers that there will be a "high threshold" for showing that tax arrangements are abusive:

"In respect of any particular arrangement there might be a range of views as to whether it was a reasonable course of action: it is possible that there could be a reasonably held view that the tax arrangements were a reasonable course of action, and also a reasonably held view that the arrangement is not a reasonable course of action. In such circumstances the tax arrangements will not be abusive for the purposes of the GAAR."

An indicator that tax arrangements may not be abusive is if they were "established practice" when entered into and HMRC indicated its acceptance of that practice at the time.

Tax arrangements may be abusive if, for example, the tax result is different to the real economic result, for example tax deductions or tax losses that are significantly greater than actual expenses or real economic losses.

If you think that all of the above is a bit vague and subjective, you are not alone. Even the best tax brains in the land don't know what this test means in practice. When legislation contains words like "reasonable" or "abusive" you have to be on your guard!

The question being asked by some tax advisers is this: will the anti-abuse rule be used to attack the sort of 'normal' or 'mainstream' tax planning carried out by thousands of small company owners, for example taking small salaries and dividends?

Many tax experts believe that well-established, conventional tax planning will not be attacked by HMRC using the GAAR. Instead the focus will be on the extreme end, for example 'aggressive' or 'artificial' tax avoidance schemes.

This view seems to be backed up by HMRC guidance published in 2015 which says the following about small company dividends:

"Just as it is essential to understand what the GAAR is targeted at, so it is equally essential to understand what it is not targeted at. To take an obvious example, a taxpayer deciding to carry on a trade can do so either as a sole trader or through a limited company whose shares he or she owns and where he or she works as an employee. Such a choice is completely outside the target area of the GAAR, and once such a company starts to earn profits a decision to accumulate most of the profits to be paid out in the future by way of dividend, rather than immediately paying a larger salary, is again something that should in any normal trading circumstances be outside the target area of the GAAR."

Nevertheless, at present the simple truth is that no one knows how HMRC will apply the general anti-abuse rule to company owners in the years ahead and whether it will eventually affect certain tax planning practices that many regard as mainstream, including some of those contained in this guide.

Changes to Personal Circumstances

It's not just changes to tax laws that could undermine the tax savings you hope to enjoy from using a company. Changes to your personal circumstances could have a similar effect.

For example, in Table 4 we saw that, at low profit levels, using a company does not save much tax.

In the worst-case scenario – if profits become losses – the company may have to start paying salaries instead of dividends (dividends require profits) and a company owner could face a significantly higher tax bill than a sole trader.

Part 5

How Couples Can Save Tax

Chapter 22

Companies Owned by Couples

So far we've compared the total tax paid by a sole trader with the total tax paid by a single company owner. But what if your spouse, common-law spouse or some other person is involved in the business?

In this chapter we compare the total tax paid by a *partnership* (two partners) with the total tax paid by two company owners.

To start with we'll assume that the company owners pay themselves tax-free salaries of £8,164 each and extract all of the remaining profits as dividends. After that we'll find out how much extra tax can be saved by reinvesting profits.

Sole traders and partnerships are taxed in pretty much the same way: each partner pays income tax and national insurance on his share of the profits. We'll assume that each partner receives 50% of the profits.

Table 8 compares the total tax (corporation tax and income tax) payable by two company owners with the total tax (income tax and national insurance) payable by two business partners.

Looking at the sample profit numbers in the table, when profits are between roughly £40,000 and £275,000 a tax saving can be achieved by using a company. For example, when profits are £100,000 a saving of £4,796 can be achieved.

However, the savings vary significantly and at many profit levels will not be sufficient to compensate for the higher costs of running a company.

The table also reveals that when profits are roughly £300,000 or higher using a company will result in an overall tax loss.

The tax savings used to be far more impressive but have been significantly reduced by the recent increase in dividend tax rates.

TABLE 8
Company vs Partnership 2017/18
Company Profits Taken as £8,164 Salary & Dividends

Profits	Company Tax	Partnership Tax	Saving
£20,000	£698	£627	-£71
£30,000	£2,598	£2,927	£329
£40,000	£4,685	£5,827	£1,142
£50,000	£7,193	£8,727	£1,534
£60,000	£9,700	£11,627	£1,927
£70,000	£12,208	£14,527	£2,319
£80,000	£14,715	£17,427	£2,712
£90,000	£17,223	£20,327	£3,104
£100,000	£19,730	£24,526	£4,796
£110,000	£22,788	£28,727	£5,938
£120,000	£27,321	£32,927	£5,606
£130,000	£31,853	£37,127	£5,273
£140,000	£36,386	£41,327	£4,941
£150,000	£40,918	£45,527	£4,608
£160,000	£45,451	£49,727	£4,276
£170,000	£49,983	£53,927	£3,943
£180,000	£54,516	£58,127	£3,611
£190,000	£59,048	£62,327	£3,278
£200,000	£63,581	£66,527	£2,946
£225,000	£74,912	£82,027	£7,115
£250,000	£87,154	£96,727	£9,573
£275,000	£102,557	£107,227	£4,669
£300,000	£118,422	£117,727	-£695
£350,000	£141,084	£141,227	£142
£400,000	£165,265	£164,727	-£538
£450,000	£190,195	£188,227	-£1,968
£500,000	£215,126	£211,727	-£3,399
£600,000	£264,987	£258,727	-£6,260
£700,000	£314,848	£305,727	-£9,121
£800,000	£364,709	£352,727	-£11,982
£900,000	£414,570	£399,727	-£14,843
£1,000,000	£464,431	£446,727	-£17,704

How the Tax Bills Are Calculated

Taking a sample profit figure from Table 8 – £100,000 – let's examine how the numbers are calculated:

Partnership Tax Calculation

Each partner pays tax on £50,000 of profits:

Income tax:	£
Profit share	50,000
Less: Personal allowance	11,500
Taxable profits	38,500
£33,500 @ 20%	6,700
£5,000 @ 40%	2,000
Total	8,700

National insurance:	
Class 2 (£2.85 x 52)	148
Class 4:	
£45,000 - £8,164 @ 9%	3,315
£50,000 - £45,000 @ 2%	100
Total	3,563

Income tax and national insurance per partner: £12,263
Combined income tax and national insurance: £24,526

Company Tax Calculation

Corporation tax:	£
Profits	100,000
Less: salaries (£8,164 x 2)	16,328
Taxable profits	83,672
Corporation tax @ 19%	15,898
After-tax profits	67,774
Dividend – each	33,887

Income tax on dividend - each:	
Remaining personal allowance (£11,500-£8,164)	3,336
Tax-free dividend allowance	5,000
Dividend taxed at 7.5% (£33,887-£3,336-£5,000)	25,551
Income tax - each	1,916

Total corporation tax and income tax: £19,730

Reinvesting Profits to Boost Tax Savings

As we know, company owners can keep profits in the company or extract them as income. Only corporation tax is payable on profits kept in the company. The company owners do not have to pay any additional income tax. By contrast, self-employed business owners pay income tax and national insurance on ALL of their profits.

Table 9 compares the total tax payable by two company owners with the total tax payable by two business partners. The company owners take a salary of £8,164 each and the rest of their income as dividends. The difference between this table and Table 8 above is that the company owners only extract 50% of the after-tax profits. The remaining profits are kept inside the company.

Once again we see that, when profits are reinvested, a company can produce bigger tax savings. For example, when profits are £100,000 the total tax saving is £7,338 (£4,796 when all profits are extracted), when profits are £200,000 the total tax saving is £27,121 (£2,946 when all profits are extracted) and when profits are £500,000 the total tax saving is £73,849 (compared with a tax *loss* of £3,399 when all profits are extracted).

Remember these are *annual savings* – it may be possible to enjoy similar savings every year.

When Reinvesting May Not Save Enough Tax

Comparing Tables 8 and 9 we can see that when profits are very low, reinvesting produces no additional tax savings. This is because reinvesting profits helps company owners save *income tax* but when profits are very low their salaries and dividends are tax free anyway thanks to the personal allowance and dividend allowance.

When profits are between around £40,000 and £70,000 using a company will produce a tax saving of between £1,329 and £3,949 when half the after-tax profits of the business are reinvested.

While these savings would be welcome, I'm not sure whether they're large enough in their own right to convince many business owners to use a company.

TABLE 9
Total Tax Bills Compared
Two Owners - 50% Profit Reinvested

Profits	Company	Partnership	Saving
£20,000	£698	£627	-£71
£30,000	£2,598	£2,927	£329
£40,000	£4,498	£5,827	£1,329
£50,000	£6,398	£8,727	£2,329
£60,000	£8,374	£11,627	£3,253
£70,000	£10,578	£14,527	£3,949
£80,000	£12,781	£17,427	£4,646
£90,000	£14,985	£20,327	£5,342
£100,000	£17,189	£24,527	£7,338
£110,000	£19,393	£28,727	£9,334
£120,000	£21,596	£32,927	£11,331
£130,000	£23,800	£37,127	£13,327
£140,000	£26,004	£41,327	£15,323
£150,000	£28,208	£45,527	£17,319
£160,000	£30,411	£49,727	£19,316
£170,000	£32,615	£53,927	£21,312
£180,000	£34,819	£58,127	£23,308
£190,000	£37,023	£62,327	£25,304
£200,000	£39,406	£66,527	£27,121
£225,000	£47,446	£82,027	£34,581
£250,000	£55,486	£96,727	£41,241
£275,000	£63,527	£107,227	£43,700
£300,000	£71,568	£117,727	£46,159
£350,000	£87,649	£141,227	£53,578
£400,000	£103,730	£164,727	£60,997
£450,000	£119,811	£188,227	£68,416
£500,000	£137,877	£211,727	£73,849
£600,000	£177,571	£258,727	£81,156
£700,000	£209,734	£305,727	£95,993
£800,000	£243,784	£352,727	£108,943
£900,000	£278,215	£399,727	£121,512
£1,000,000	£312,645	£446,727	£134,082

How the Tax Bills Are Calculated

Taking a sample profit figure from Table 9 – £200,000 – let's examine how the company tax numbers are calculated (the partnership figures are the same as in Table 8):

Company Tax Calculation

Corporation tax:	£
Profits	200,000
Less: salaries (£8,164 x 2)	16,328
Taxable profits	183,672
Corporation tax @ 19%	34,898
After-tax profits	148,774

After-tax profits:	£
Reinvested (£148,774 x 50%)	74,387
Dividends	74,387
Dividend – each (£74,387/2)	37,194

Income tax on dividend – each:	
Remaining personal allowance:	
(£11,500 - £8,164 salary)	3,336
Dividend allowance	5,000
Total tax-free dividend	8,336
Remaining taxable dividend	28,858
Basic-rate band (£33,500-£5,000)	28,500
Basic-rate tax @ 7.5%	2,138
Taxed at higher rate	358
Higher-rate tax @ 32.5%	116
Total income tax	2,254

Income tax – combined	
£2,254 x 2	4,508

Total corporation tax and income tax: £39,406

A partnership with identical profits will pay £66,527 in tax.

One Shareholder versus Two Shareholders

So far we've compared the tax paid by company owners with the tax paid by sole traders and partnerships.

Another interesting question is:

How much tax is saved if a company has two owners instead of one?

Table 10 compares the total tax (corporation tax and income tax) payable by one company owner with the total tax payable by two company owners.

The figures come from Table 8 above and Table 4 in Chapter 13.

Clearly, involving your spouse/partner in the business could produce significant additional tax savings. For example, if profits are £50,000 your spouse could save you £2,672 in tax. If profits are £100,000 your spouse could save you £12,060 in tax!

The basic idea is that, by involving your spouse/partner, you can benefit from two tax-free salaries and two lots of dividends that are either tax-free or taxed at just 7.5%. By splitting your income it also takes longer to reach the £100,000 and £150,000 thresholds where extortionate tax rates kick in.

Note that the tax savings will be smaller or disappear altogether if your spouse/partner has income from other sources, e.g. another job or business or portfolio of rental properties.

Furthermore, when it comes to paying salaries and dividends to your spouse there are certain traps you have to watch out for, as we shall see in the next chapter.

TABLE 10
One versus Two Company Owners
Profits Taken as £8,164 Salary & Dividends

Profits	One Owner	Two Owners	Saving
£20,000	£2,343	£698	£1,645
£30,000	£4,850	£2,598	£2,252
£40,000	£7,358	£4,685	£2,672
£50,000	£9,865	£7,193	£2,672
£60,000	£13,660	£9,700	£3,960
£70,000	£18,193	£12,208	£5,985
£80,000	£22,725	£14,715	£8,010
£90,000	£27,258	£17,223	£10,035
£100,000	£31,790	£19,730	£12,060
£110,000	£36,323	£22,788	£13,535
£120,000	£40,855	£27,321	£13,535
£130,000	£46,512	£31,853	£14,659
£140,000	£52,867	£36,386	£16,482
£150,000	£59,211	£40,918	£18,293
£160,000	£63,743	£45,451	£18,293
£170,000	£68,276	£49,983	£18,293
£180,000	£72,808	£54,516	£18,293
£190,000	£77,646	£59,048	£18,598
£200,000	£82,632	£63,581	£19,051
£225,000	£95,098	£74,912	£20,185
£250,000	£107,563	£87,154	£20,409
£275,000	£120,028	£102,557	£17,471
£300,000	£132,493	£118,422	£14,071
£350,000	£157,424	£141,084	£16,339
£400,000	£182,354	£165,265	£17,090
£450,000	£207,285	£190,195	£17,090
£500,000	£232,215	£215,126	£17,090
£600,000	£282,076	£264,987	£17,090
£700,000	£331,937	£314,848	£17,090
£800,000	£381,798	£364,709	£17,090
£900,000	£431,659	£414,570	£17,090
£1,000,000	£481,520	£464,431	£17,090

Potential Tax Savings in 2020/21

Finally, let's move forward to the 2020/21 tax year when the corporation tax rate is expected to fall to 17%.

Tables 11 and 12 compare the total tax (corporation tax and income tax) payable by two company owners with the total tax (income tax and national insurance) payable by two business partners.

In Table 11 it's assumed that the company owners extract all the profits, in Table 12 it's assumed they extract just 50%.

Assumptions

As before the numbers in Tables 11 and 12 are calculated by making the following assumptions:

- Corporation tax is reduced to 17%
- The income tax higher-rate threshold is £50,000
- The personal allowance is £12,500
- Class 2 national insurance is abolished
- The national insurance threshold is £8,750
- The dividend allowance is £2,000
- All other tax rates/rules remain the same.

What do the tables reveal? Comparing Table 8 (the current tax year) with Table 11 (2020/21) it's clear that at many profit levels using a company will become more attractive, even when all profits are extracted from the business. For example, two company owners with profits of £250,000 currently pay £9,573 less tax than two partners – in 2020/21 they could pay £12,968 less tax.

However, the additional tax savings are not this impressive at all profit levels and when profits are very high company owners will pay more tax than partnerships.

Looking at Table 12 we once again see that using a company should continue to be very attractive when profits are reinvested. For example, two company owners with profits of £250,000 will pay £46,029 less tax than two partners if 50% of the after-tax profits are reinvested. However, when profits are relatively low (e.g. less than £50,000) the savings are modest or do not exist.

TABLE 11
Company vs Partnership 2020/21
Company Profits Taken as £8,750 Salary & Dividends

Profits	Company Tax	Partnership Tax	Saving
£20,000	£425	£225	-£200
£30,000	£2,125	£2,125	£0
£40,000	£4,363	£5,025	£662
£50,000	£6,686	£7,925	£1,239
£60,000	£9,008	£10,825	£1,817
£70,000	£11,331	£13,725	£2,394
£80,000	£13,653	£16,625	£2,972
£90,000	£15,976	£19,525	£3,549
£100,000	£18,298	£22,425	£4,127
£110,000	£20,621	£26,625	£6,004
£120,000	£23,587	£30,825	£7,238
£130,000	£27,984	£35,025	£7,041
£140,000	£32,382	£39,225	£6,843
£150,000	£36,779	£43,425	£6,646
£160,000	£41,177	£47,625	£6,448
£170,000	£45,574	£51,825	£6,251
£180,000	£49,972	£56,025	£6,053
£190,000	£54,369	£60,225	£5,856
£200,000	£58,767	£64,425	£5,658
£225,000	£69,761	£79,925	£10,164
£250,000	£82,457	£95,425	£12,968
£275,000	£97,836	£105,925	£8,089
£300,000	£113,054	£116,425	£3,371
£350,000	£135,042	£139,925	£4,883
£400,000	£158,988	£163,425	£4,437
£450,000	£183,299	£186,925	£3,626
£500,000	£207,611	£210,425	£2,814
£600,000	£256,234	£257,425	£1,191
£700,000	£304,857	£304,425	-£432
£800,000	£353,480	£351,425	-£2,055
£900,000	£402,103	£398,425	-£3,678
£1,000,000	£450,726	£445,425	-£5,301

TABLE 12
Company vs Partnership 2020/21
50% Profits Reinvested

Profits	Company Tax	Partnership Tax	Saving
£20,000	£425	£225	-£200
£30,000	£2,125	£2,125	£0
£40,000	£3,825	£5,025	£1,200
£50,000	£5,674	£7,925	£2,251
£60,000	£7,685	£10,825	£3,140
£70,000	£9,697	£13,725	£4,028
£80,000	£11,708	£16,625	£4,917
£90,000	£13,719	£19,525	£5,806
£100,000	£15,730	£22,425	£6,695
£110,000	£17,742	£26,625	£8,883
£120,000	£19,753	£30,825	£11,072
£130,000	£21,764	£35,025	£13,261
£140,000	£23,775	£39,225	£15,450
£150,000	£25,787	£43,425	£17,638
£160,000	£27,798	£47,625	£19,827
£170,000	£29,809	£51,825	£22,016
£180,000	£31,820	£56,025	£24,205
£190,000	£33,832	£60,225	£26,393
£200,000	£35,843	£64,425	£28,582
£225,000	£41,774	£79,925	£38,151
£250,000	£49,396	£95,425	£46,029
£275,000	£57,018	£105,925	£48,907
£300,000	£64,640	£116,425	£51,785
£350,000	£79,883	£139,925	£60,042
£400,000	£95,127	£163,425	£68,298
£450,000	£110,371	£186,925	£76,554
£500,000	£128,668	£210,425	£81,757
£600,000	£166,415	£257,425	£91,010
£700,000	£196,943	£304,425	£107,482
£800,000	£229,755	£351,425	£121,670
£900,000	£262,566	£398,425	£135,859
£1,000,000	£295,378	£445,425	£150,047

Chapter 23

Splitting Income: Practical Issues

In Chapter 22 it was shown that a couple may be able to double up the tax-free salary and low-taxed dividend.

That's all very well if the couple own and run the company together. But what if your spouse/partner isn't involved in the business, for example if the company was started before you met or if they have a separate career and receive salary income from another employer?

In situations like these it may still be possible to save income tax by gifting shares in the company to your spouse. It may even be possible to save tax by paying them a salary as well.

The amount of tax that can be saved depends on individual circumstances, for example how much profit the company makes and how much taxable income each person has already.

Tax savings are typically achieved where one spouse is a higher-rate taxpayer (paying 32.5% tax on their dividend income) and the other spouse has no income at all or is a basic-rate taxpayer.

However, it's not just these couples who can save tax. It's possible to pay income tax at more than 32.5% on dividend income that falls into any of the following tax brackets:

- £50,000-£60,000   Child benefit charge
- £100,000-£123,000   Personal allowance withdrawal
- Over £150,000   Additional-rate tax

If your income falls into one of these tax brackets you may be able to save tax by transferring income to your spouse, even if your spouse is a higher-rate taxpayer.

And because every taxpayer is entitled to a dividend allowance, it may be possible to save tax by shifting some dividend income to your spouse/partner, even if they're in the same tax bracket as you or even a higher tax bracket. Unfortunately, the potential tax savings will be relatively modest in future because the dividend allowance is being reduced from £5,000 to £2,000 in April 2018

Before we look at some sample tax savings it is important to point out that there are also potential dangers when it comes to splitting income with your spouse in this fashion. We will return to this important issue later in the chapter.

Capital Gains Tax

If you wish to split your dividend income with your spouse you generally have to transfer shares in the company to them.

In the case of married couples, a gift of shares would be exempt from capital gains tax.

Gifts between unmarried couples are normally subject to capital gains tax. However, the couple may be able to jointly elect to claim holdover relief.

Holdover relief allows a chargeable gain to be deferred (held over) when gifts of qualifying business assets are made. The person who receives the shares may eventually have to pay capital gains tax on your gain as well as their own when the shares are sold.

To qualify for holdover relief the company must generally be a regular trading company.

Unmarried couples who want to split their income face a further potential danger (see below).

Giving the Business Away

To successfully split your dividend income with your spouse it is essential that proper ownership of shares in the company is handed over. This means your spouse must be able to do what they like with any dividends paid out and with any capital growth from any sale of the business.

As we shall see shortly, it is also safer to transfer ordinary shares rather than shares that have fewer voting rights or other rights.

It's probably advisable to have your spouse's dividends paid into a separate bank account in their name, to illustrate to HMRC that you have not retained control of the money.

Dividends are generally payable in proportion to shareholdings. So if you normally take a dividend of £100,000 and want to transfer £40,000 of this income to your spouse, you will generally have to transfer 40% of the business to them.

Because this sort of tax planning, if done correctly, involves effectively giving away ownership and control of part of your business, it is only suitable where there is a significant amount of trust between the parties involved.

How Much of the Business Should Be Transferred?

For many company owners, a 50:50 ownership split with their spouse/partner is optimal, but a smaller stake can be transferred if the founder wants to retain more control of the business.

Spouse Has No Taxable Income

If you are a basic-rate taxpayer (income under £45,000 in 2017/18) and your spouse is a 'house-spouse' with no taxable income, they can receive tax-free dividends of up to £16,500 in 2017/18 (made up of the £11,500 personal allowance and £5,000 dividend allowance). The potential tax saving is £1,238 (£16,500 x 7.5%).

If you are a higher-rate taxpayer and your spouse has no taxable income, they can receive less heavily taxed dividends of up to £45,000 in 2017/18. The first £16,500 will be tax free and £2,138 tax will be payable on the remaining £28,500 (at 7.5%).

Because you would pay £14,625 tax on the same income (£45,000 x 32.5%) the potential tax saving is £12,487 (£14,625 - £2,138).

The tax saving could be even greater if taking more dividend income would push your income over the £100,000 threshold where your personal allowance would be withdrawn.

Spouse is a Basic-Rate Taxpayer

Even if your spouse works and has taxable income, it may be possible to save tax by gifting shares in the business to them. Again, the tax savings will vary from case to case.

Example
Rupert is a company owner who expects to have a taxable income of £60,000 in 2017/18, made up of a £50,000 dividend and £10,000 of salary and other income. He will pay 32.5% tax on £15,000 of his dividend income (£60,000 - £45,000 higher-rate threshold).

His wife Wendy receives income of £30,000 from another source. Thus she has £15,000 of her basic-rate band left and can receive up to £15,000 of dividend income that will be less heavily taxed in her hands.

If Rupert gifts 25% of the shares to Wendy and the company normally pays dividends of £50,000, she'll receive £12,500. The first £5,000 will currently be tax free thanks to the dividend allowance and tax of £563 will be payable on the remaining £7,500 (at 7.5%). Rupert would've paid £4,063 tax on this income (at 32.5%) so the tax saving is £3,500.

Spouse is a Higher-Rate Taxpayer

If you and your spouse/partner are both higher-rate taxpayers (income over £45,000 in 2017/18) it may still possible to save tax by gifting them shares in the company. Not only does your spouse have their own dividend allowance but evening up your income may help you avoid the child benefit charge.

Example revisited
The facts are exactly the same as before except Wendy's income is £45,000 instead of £30,000 and she receives £1,789 child benefit for two children. As things stand, the couple's child benefit will be completely withdrawn because Rupert's income is £60,000.

If Rupert gifts 15% of the business to Wendy she'll get dividends of £7,500 and his income will fall to £52,500. She'll pay no tax on the first £5,000 this year. Rupert would pay 32.5%, so the saving is £1,625.

She'll pay 32.5% tax on the other £2,500 but her income is now £52,500, the same as Rupert's. By equalising incomes the couple will be able to hold onto ¾ of their child benefit – a saving of £1,342 this year.

Why the Tax Savings May Not Last

There are many reasons why any tax savings that may be achieved in one tax year by splitting income with your spouse may not be achievable in full in future tax years, including:

- Changes to tax rates and thresholds
- Changes to personal circumstances

Changes to Tax Rates & Thresholds

The dividend allowance will be cut from £5,000 to £2,000 in April 2018. This will reduce the tax savings that may be achieved by shifting dividends to a spouse who is in the same tax bracket as you, for example where you are both higher-rate taxpayers.

If the additional rate (income over £150,000) is eventually abolished this will eliminate most of the savings that can be achieved by shifting dividends to a higher-rate taxpayer.

Further changes that eliminate tax savings cannot be ruled out.

Changes to Personal Circumstances

Because every taxpayer can benefit from the dividend allowance (£5,000 this year, £2,000 next year) it is possible to save some tax by shifting income to your spouse, even if your spouse pays tax at a higher rate than you.

Beyond the dividend allowance, income tax savings can generally only be achieved if your spouse has a lower tax rate than you.

It is possible that, over time, your tax rate will fall or your spouse's tax rate will increase. This could eliminate or even reverse any initial income tax saving that is achieved.

Your tax rate could fall if the company's profits fall, resulting in lower dividends. Your spouse's tax rate could rise if their income from other sources increases. There are lots of different permutations. The key point is that couples should look further ahead than just one year when deciding what proportion of the company each should own.

HMRC's Attacks on Income Shifting

Income splitting arrangements like those described in this chapter have come under attack in recent years. In particular, the taxman has tried to prevent dividends being paid to non-working spouses or spouses who do just a small amount of work for the company.

In particular, the taxman's target has been small 'personal service' companies (IT consultants and the like) where most of the work is carried out by one person.

It all came to a head in the notorious 'Arctic Systems' tax case. HMRC tried to use the so-called settlements legislation to prevent Geoff Jones, a computer consultant, from splitting his dividend income with his wife.

The settlements legislation is designed to prevent income being shifted from one individual to another via a 'settlement', e.g. by transferring an asset or making some other 'arrangement'.

In the Arctic Systems case Mr Jones did most of the work in the company. Mrs Jones did a few hours admin each week. Because Mr Jones only paid himself a small salary despite all the work he did, more money was left to pay out as dividends to Mrs Jones. HMRC therefore decided that a settlement had taken place and tried to have Mrs Jones' dividend income taxed in her husband's hands.

HMRC originally won the case but the decision was overturned by the House of Lords.

The judges agreed with HMRC that a settlement had taken place **but** decided that the settlement provisions could not be applied because in this case the couple were protected by the exemption for gifts between spouses. This exemption applies where:

- There is an outright gift of property to a spouse, and
- The property is not wholly or mainly a right to income

On the first point, the judges ruled that, although Mrs Jones had subscribed for her share when the company was set up (i.e., it was not strictly speaking gifted to her by her husband), her share was essentially a gift because it contained an 'element of bounty': the share provided a benefit that Mr Jones would not have given to a complete stranger.

On the second point, the judges also ruled that a gift of *ordinary* shares is not wholly or mainly a right to income because ordinary shares have other rights: voting rights and the right to capital gains if the company is sold.

Thanks to the courage of Mr and Mrs Jones, who were prepared to fight HMRC all the way to the House of Lords, this exemption should safeguard most types of income splitting arrangements between married couples where ordinary shares are involved.

For this reason many tax advisers are of the opinion that married couples should make hay while the sun shines, i.e. they should split their dividend income with their spouses while they can.

Preference Shares

The outcome of the Arctic Systems case may have been different if another type of share other than ordinary shares had been involved.

In another tax case (*Young v Pearce*), wives were issued with preference shares that paid income but had very few other rights. The shares did not have voting rights and did not entitle the spouses to receive any payout in the event of the company being sold (other than the original £25 payment for the shares).

All that the preference shares provided was a right to receive 30% of the company's profits as a dividend. The court therefore decided the preference shares provided wholly or mainly a right to income. Thus the exemption for gifts between spouses was not available and the settlement rules applied. The wives' dividends were therefore taxed in the hands of their husbands.

Unmarried Couples & Other Family Members

Although HMRC was defeated in the Arctic Systems case, the judges agreed that a settlement had taken place. The taxpayers only won thanks to the exemption for gifts between *spouses*.

There is still uncertainty as to where this leaves income-splitting arrangements between other groups of individuals, in particular, *unmarried* couples.

HMRC probably does take the view that the settlements legislation applies to unmarried couples and other family members, especially where small personal service companies are involved.

However, to date the taxman has not pursued these individuals aggressively so, again, it may be a case of making hay while the sun shines.

To protect against any potential attack the best defence is probably to have both individuals equally involved in the business (a bit of admin or bookkeeping will not suffice, as Mr and Mrs Jones discovered.)

HMRC's main concern seems to be personal service companies (IT consultants and other businesses where the profits are generated from one person's services). Larger businesses that have other employees, premises, equipment etc may be safer because the profits come from various sources, not just one person's work.

Danger Ahead?

In 2007 draft income shifting legislation was published but fortunately never made it onto the statute books after being widely condemned for being completely unworkable.

That draft legislation essentially sought to prevent business owners from receiving dividends unless they effectively earned them! This would have undermined the whole basis of shareholder capitalism – dividends are supposed to be a reward for being an entrepreneur and setting up or investing in a business.

Although income shifting legislation is on the back burner for now, it could be introduced in the future and could upset some income splitting arrangements.

Salaries for Spouses

If your partner also works for your company they can be paid a salary. Please note, you cannot pay them a salary if they do no work for the company. And you cannot pay them more than the market rate. If you do, the company will be denied tax relief for the expense.

If your partner has no taxable income from other sources, a small salary will be more tax efficient than simply paying them dividends. Why? Unlike dividends which are paid out of the company's after-tax profits, salaries are a tax deductible expense for the company. In other words, in addition to any *income tax* savings enjoyed by the couple, a salary will also save the company *corporation tax*.

For example, a small salary of £8,164 will save a company £1,551 in corporation tax (at 19%).

To avoid national insurance salary payments should be made monthly instead of as a lump sum. If, however, your spouse is a director the payment can be made as a lump sum because company directors pay national insurance on an annual basis.

Second Jobs

What if your spouse already has income from other sources, e.g. a salary from another job? Is it still tax efficient to get your company to pay them a small salary?

Firstly, it's important to point out that, if your spouse works for another employer, the employment contract may prevent them working for you as well.

If there is no such restriction, paying your spouse a small salary could lead to an overall saving of several hundred pounds in some cases. Why? Because for basic-rate taxpayers the combined tax rate (corporation tax and income tax) for dividend income is now roughly 25%, compared with 20% for salaries.

Thus paying your spouse a salary of, say, £8,164 could lead to an overall saving of just over £400 (£8,164 x 5%), providing there is no national insurance payable.

The savings may be much smaller or non-existent in other cases, for example for some higher-rate taxpayers, so it may be necessary to do some calculations specific to your circumstances.

Part 6

Controlling Your Tax Bill

Chapter 24

Company Owners Can Control Their Income Tax Bills

A company owner can often decide whether any distribution of the company's money is classified as salary or dividend.

Another advantage of being a company owner is that you have complete control over how much income you withdraw in total.

This gives you significant control over your personal income tax bill.

Unlike sole traders, who pay tax each year on ALL the profits of the business, company owners only pay income tax on the money they actually withdraw from the company.

This allows company owners to reduce their income tax bills by adopting the following strategies:

- 'Smooth income'
- 'Roller-coaster income'

Smooth Income

With smooth income, the company owner withdraws roughly the same amount of money each year, even though the company's profits may fluctuate considerably.

'Smooth income' allows the director/shareholder to stay below any of the following key income tax thresholds that could result in a higher income tax bill:

- £45,000   Higher-rate tax
- £50,000   Child benefit tax charge
- £100,000   Personal allowance withdrawal
- £150,000   Additional rate tax

The last three thresholds didn't even exist a few years ago, which goes to show how much more complicated and burdensome the UK's income tax system has become for those considered to be 'high earners'.

Roller-coaster Income

With 'roller-coaster income', the company owners take a bigger or smaller salary or dividend than would normally be required to fund their lifestyles.

Roller-coaster income could save you tax in the following circumstances:

Tax Rates Are Going Up Or Down

If the Government announces that tax rates will rise during a future tax year, you may wish to pay yourself more income now and less income later on.

And if your tax rate will *fall* during a future tax year, you should pay yourself less income now and more income later on.

You Want to Avoid Capital Gains Tax

It may also make sense for company owners to pay themselves less income during tax years in which they sell assets subject to capital gains tax, e.g. rental properties.

Why? This may allow some of your basic-rate band (£33,500 in 2017/18) to be freed up, which means some of your capital gains will be taxed at 10% or 18% instead of 20% or 28%.

Pension Income

When you reach age 55 you may decide to start withdrawing money from any private pension scheme you belong to, for example a self-invested personal pension (SIPP). Any amount you withdraw over and above your 25% tax-free lump sum will be subject to income tax.

Fortunately, with a drawdown arrangement you can vary the amount of income you withdraw from your pension scheme every year and there are no limits placed on the amount of income you can withdraw.

Coupled with the fact that you can vary the amount of income you withdraw from your company, this could allow you to minimise your income tax bill by staying below any of the income tax thresholds listed earlier.

Chapter 25

Using a Company to Protect Your Child Benefit

Child benefit is gradually withdrawn where any member of a household has over £50,000 income. This is done by imposing a High Income Child Benefit Charge on the highest earner in the household.

Once the highest earner's income reaches £60,000, all of the child benefit will effectively have been taken away in higher tax charges.

The £50,000 threshold can be increased or decreased by the Government but will not automatically increase with inflation. In other words, over time more and more taxpayers may face paying the new child benefit tax charge.

Company owners can avoid the child benefit charge by altering the amount of income they extract from their companies. In other words, they can keep their incomes below £50,000 in some or all tax years. Self-employed business owners cannot do this.

Child Benefit: How Much is it Worth?

Child benefit is an extremely valuable *tax-free* handout from the Government. Parents who qualify currently receive:

- £1,076.40 for the first child
- £712.40 for each subsequent child

Depending on the number of children, a family can expect to receive the following total child benefit payment:

Children	Total Child Benefit
1	£1,076
2	£1,789
3	£2,501
4	£3,214

plus £712.40 for each additional child

How Long Do Child Benefit Payments Continue?

Child benefit generally continues to be paid until your children are 16 years old.

The payments will continue until age 20 if the child is enrolled in full-time 'non-advanced' education, including:

- GCSEs
- A levels
- Scottish Highers
- NVQ/SVQ level 1, 2 or 3
- BTEC National Diploma, National Certificate, 1st Diploma

So if your child is 16, 17, 18 or 19 and enrolled in one of the above courses, child benefit will continue to be paid.

Once the child is 20 years old all child benefit payments will cease.

The following courses do NOT qualify:

- Degrees
- Diploma of Higher Education
- NVQ level 4 or above
- HNCs or HNDs
- Teacher training

In other words, if your children are 16, 17, 18 or 19 and enrolled in any these courses, you will not receive any child benefit.

Total Value of Child Benefit

Child benefit payments continue for between 16 and 20 years. Based on current child benefit rates, the total amount you can expect to receive over the total period your child qualifies is:

- £17,222 to £21,528 tax free for the first child
- £11,398 to £14,248 tax free for each additional child

These are very much 'back of the envelope' figures because they ignore the potential danger that child benefit may not hold its real value if it is frozen or doesn't increase in line inflation.

However, they clearly illustrate how valuable child benefit is over many years and why it is worth protecting where possible.

The £50,000 Threshold for Company Owners

To avoid the child benefit charge you have to keep your salary and dividends below £50,000.

In previous chapters we have shown that company owners can pay themselves income of up to £45,000 before becoming higher-rate taxpayers and paying 32.5% tax on their dividends.

This leaves you scope to pay an additional dividend of £5,000 before the child benefit charge comes into force. The total income tax payable on the additional dividend will be £1,625 (£5,000 x 32.5%).

A company owner who takes a salary of £8,164 and wants to avoid the child benefit charge in 2017/18 can take a dividend of £41,836 (£8,336 will be tax free, £28,500 will be taxed at 7.5% and £5,000 at 32.5%). Total taxable income: £50,000. Total after-tax income: £46,237.

For a company owned and managed by a couple, the above amounts can be doubled up. Total after-tax income: £92,474.

Income between £50,000 and £60,000

If you want to extract more income from your company you will face paying the High Income Child Benefit Charge.

For every £100 of income over £50,000 a tax charge equivalent to 1% of the child benefit is levied on the highest earner in the household.

For example, if the highest earner in the household has income of £55,000, the tax charge will be equivalent to 50% of the child benefit claimed.

If the highest earner in the household has income of £60,000 or more, the tax charge will be 100% of the child benefit claimed.

For the highest earner in the household the child benefit charge creates the following marginal tax rates on dividend income in the £50,000-£60,000 tax bracket:

Children	Marginal Tax Rate on Cash Dividends
1	43%
2	50%
3	58%
4	65%

Plus 7% for each additional child.

Example

David, a company owner, has taken a salary and dividends totalling £50,000 so far in 2017/18. He is the highest earner in a household claiming child benefit for two children.

David decides to withdraw additional dividend income of £10,000. His total income will be £60,000 so he will face the maximum child benefit charge. The tax payable on the additional dividend is £5,039, calculated as follows:

£10,000 dividend x 32.5%	*£3,250*
£1,789 child benefit x 100%	*£1,789*
Total additional tax	*£5,039*

The effective tax rate on the additional £10,000 dividend is 50.39%.

Income between £60,000 and £100,000

If your income exceeds £60,000 you will already be paying the maximum child benefit charge. Income between £60,000 and £100,000 does not incur any further child benefit charge. Dividends between £60,000 and £100,000 will continue to be taxed at 32.5%.

Once your income rises above £100,000 you face a fresh tax sting: withdrawal of the income tax personal allowance.

How to Avoid the Child Benefit Charge

Clearly taxpayers have an enormous incentive to escape the higher tax rates that apply to dividends in the £50,000-£60,000 bracket. Company owners may find it easier than other taxpayers to escape the child benefit charge because they can alter the amount of dividend income they receive each year.

Some company owners may be able to avoid the charge altogether by keeping their income below £50,000. Others, including those who usually withdraw more than £60,000 each year, may be able to avoid the charge in some tax years but not others, or partly reduce the charge.

Company owners can also spread their income among family members, for example, by gifting shares in the business to their spouses.

For the current and future tax years, the following dividend strategies could be considered:

Smooth Income

If the income you withdraw is currently somewhere between the higher-rate threshold (£45,000) and £50,000, and you expect your income to continue growing above £50,000, you could consider extracting approximately £50,000 for several tax years, where possible. This may mean you pay yourself more income than you need to begin with and less income than you need later on, but by doing so you may be able to avoid the child benefit charge completely for several years.

Roller-Coaster Income

If you plan to withdraw *more than* £60,000 from 2017/18 onwards, you could consider taking big dividends during some tax years and smaller ones in other tax years.

For example, instead of taking £75,000 every year, consider taking £100,000 every second year, if possible, and £50,000 in the intervening years. This will allow you to avoid the child benefit charge every second year.

Similarly, a company owner who normally takes £60,000 every year could consider taking £70,000 in year 1 and £50,000 in year 2, where possible.

Austerity

If your taxable income is normally over £50,000, you could consider keeping your income below £50,000 for several years to avoid the child benefit charge.

For example, let's say you have three children and your taxable income is normally £60,000. If for the next three years you can afford to withdraw just £50,000, you may be able to protect over £7,500 of child benefit.

Other Issues

When paying yourself dividends that are smaller than normal or bigger than normal there may be lots of other issues to consider.

For example, you can only declare bigger dividends if the company has sufficient distributable profits.

If you postpone taking some of your dividends until a future tax year, you may leave yourself exposed to any future increase in tax on company owners. Remember tax rules are constantly changing.

If you take a smaller than normal dividend this may have other financial repercussions, for example it may affect the size of mortgage you are able to get.

Chapter 26

Business Owners with Income from Other Sources

Introduction

Company owners deciding how much income to withdraw from their companies need to be aware of the following income tax thresholds and brackets:

- Over £45,000   Higher rate tax
- £50,000-£60,000   Child benefit tax charge
- £100,000-£123,000   Personal allowance withdrawal
- Over £150,000   Additional rate of tax

If your total taxable income is less than £45,000 you'll pay no more than 7.5% income tax on your dividends. Once your income exceeds £45,000, you start paying tax at 32.5%.

However, income that falls into the final three tax brackets is taxed at much higher rates:

- £50,000-£60,000   43% to 65% or more
- £100,000-£123,000   53% in some cases
- Over £150,000   38.1%

(Note: the £50,000-£60,000 threshold only applies to households in receipt of child benefit.)

When trying to avoid these extortionate tax rates, you must remember to include any other taxable income you receive. Income from other sources could force your company income, in particular your dividend income, into a higher tax bracket.

To avoid a potential tax sting you may wish to reduce the amount of income you withdraw from your company. Company owners can vary their income from year to year but the self-employed (sole traders and partnerships) have far less flexibility. Being able to control your taxable income is one of the major benefits of using a company.

The Order in which Income is Taxed

Income is taxed in the following order:

- Non-savings income:
  - ➢ Employment income
  - ➢ Self-employment income
  - ➢ Rental income
- Savings income
- Dividend income

Dividends are always treated as the top slice of income.

Let's say you expect to earn £10,000 of rental income during the current tax year but, so far, have not withdrawn any income from your company. As things stand, all of your rental income will be tax free, being covered by your income tax personal allowance.

Let's say you now decide to withdraw a salary of £11,500 and a dividend of £33,500 from your company (the maximum amount you can withdraw tax free or taxed at just 7.5%, in the absence of any other income).

The decision to take a salary means you now have £21,500 of non-savings income and your income tax bill will increase by £2,000:

£21,500 - £11,500 personal allowance = £10,000 x 20% = £2,000

Effectively, you've paid 20% tax on your salary.

And what about your dividends which are supposedly taxed at no more than 7.5%?

Thanks to your rental income, £10,000 of your dividend income will now be pushed into the higher-rate tax bracket and taxed at 32.5% instead of 7.5%, resulting in additional tax of £2,500.

In summary, having £10,000 of rental income increases the company owner's tax bill by £4,500!

Income from Other Sources

With the exception of self-employment income, it may be possible to extract all of the various types of income listed above from your own company: employment income, rental income, interest income, and dividend income.

We've already talked extensively about salaries (employment income) and dividends. If your company uses a property that you own personally (for example, an office or shop) it can also pay you rent. And if your company borrows money from you it can pay you interest.

In this chapter the focus is on company owners who have income from *other sources* – i.e. income that does not come out of their own company.

More specifically, the focus is on company owners who have income from other sources that is subject to *income tax*.

Some income (e.g. most interest income and stock market dividends) can be sheltered from income tax inside an ISA or pension scheme.

It is also possible to shelter assets from income tax inside another company. Some property investors do this. Corporation tax is still payable on any rental profits produced by the properties but the income tax position of the director/shareholder will be unaffected, unless those profits are extracted.

Those company owners who do have a significant amount of taxable income from other sources, and cannot shelter it from income tax, may wish to reduce the amount of income they withdraw from their own companies, so as to avoid paying income tax at some of the extortionate rates listed at the beginning of this chapter.

Other Income – Control

One of the benefits of being a company owner is that you can control how much income you withdraw from your business. This allows you to control your income tax bill from year to year.

Income from other sources is often less easy to control. For example, it may not be possible to shift it from one tax year into another tax year.

You may be able to control the dividends declared by your own company but you cannot force the board of BT to increase or lower its dividend!

Company owners who want to keep their taxable income just below any of the key income tax thresholds may therefore have to increase or decrease their *company income* – it may not always be possible to alter the amount of income you receive from other sources.

Table 13 shows the maximum dividend you can withdraw during 2017/18 if you have other taxable income (including employment income) and want to avoid some of the key income tax thresholds.

For example, if you have other taxable income of £20,000 a dividend of £25,000 will keep your income below £45,000 and you will avoid paying 32.5% tax.

A dividend of up to £30,000 will ensure that your income does not exceed £50,000. Some of your dividend income will be taxed at 32.5% but you will avoid the child benefit tax charge.

A dividend of up to £80,000 will ensure that your income does not exceed £100,000. A significant amount of your dividend income will be taxed at 32.5% and you may end up paying the maximum child benefit tax charge but you will not lose any of your personal allowance.

Table 13 is also relevant to Scottish taxpayers.

TABLE 13
Avoiding the Tax Thresholds
Maximum Dividend 2017/18

Other Income	Threshold £45,000	£50,000	£100,000
£8,164	£36,836	£41,836	£91,836
£11,500	£33,500	£38,500	£88,500
£15,000	£30,000	£35,000	£85,000
£20,000	£25,000	£30,000	£80,000
£25,000	£20,000	£25,000	£75,000
£30,000	£15,000	£20,000	£70,000
£35,000	£10,000	£15,000	£65,000
£40,000	£5,000	£10,000	£60,000

Note: First £5,000 of dividend income tax free

Remember, no matter how much other income you have, you can always receive at least some tax-free dividend income each year. This is thanks to the dividend allowance which is £5,000 this year but just £2,000 from 2018/19 onwards.

For example, someone with other income of £45,000 can still receive a tax-free dividend of £5,000 this year without having to worry about paying 32.5% tax.

In some cases, taking tax-free dividend income will have other negative tax consequences.

For example, someone with other income of £50,000 can receive £5,000 of tax-free dividend income. However, this will bring their total income to £55,000 which means they could end up paying half the maximum child benefit charge.

Someone with other income of £100,000 can receive £5,000 of tax-free dividend income. However, this will bring their total income to £105,000 which means they will lose £2,500 of their personal allowance. This in turn will increase the income tax on their other income by £1,000 (£2,500 x 40%).

Other Income –Predictability

At the start of a new tax year you may not know with complete certainty how much taxable income you will receive from other sources during the year. This could be problematic if you wish to withdraw dividends from your company *at the beginning of the tax year*.

If you withdraw dividends from your company and your other income then turns out to be higher than expected, you may end up paying more income tax than you expected on your company dividends.

Some types of income are, however, more predictable than others. For example, interest income, stock market dividends and rental income are arguably more predictable than, say, the profits of a sole trader business (self-employment income).

Some types of income, if not completely predictable, are more likely to end up being *less than expected*, rather than higher than expected. For example, a rental property that normally generates rental income of £1,000 per month may lie empty for three months, thereby producing an annual income of £9,000 rather than £12,000.

If your income from other sources turns out to be less than expected, you may be able to get your company to pay you additional dividend income before the end of the tax year.

If your income from other sources turns out to be *higher than expected* you generally cannot reverse any dividends you have already taken out of your company.

Company owners who have unpredictable income from other sources may therefore wish to postpone paying dividends until closer to the end of the tax year, if they are concerned that their dividend income may fall into a heavily taxed bracket.

Chapter 27

How to Pay Less CGT by Postponing Dividends

The main capital gains tax rates were reduced in April 2016:

- From 18% to 10%   Basic rate taxpayers
- From 28% to 20%   Higher rate taxpayers

Sadly, the 18% and 28% rates still apply to gains arising on disposals of residential property.

Where the individual is entitled to Entrepreneurs Relief, the gain is taxed at 10%. Entrepreneurs Relief is generally only available when you sell or wind up a business. In all other cases, the amount of capital gains tax you pay depends on how much income you have earned during the tax year.

In the absence of Entrepreneurs Relief, the maximum amount of capital gains that you can have taxed at 10% or 18% during the current tax year is £33,500. This is the amount of the basic-rate tax band for 2017/18.

Basic-rate taxpayers pay 10% less capital gains tax than higher-rate taxpayers. This means the basic-rate tax band can save each person up to £3,350 in capital gains tax this year:

£33,500 x 10% = £3,350

This creates some interesting tax-planning opportunities:

Income Planning

If you expect to realise a large capital gain, for example by disposing of a buy-to-let property, you may be able to save quite a lot of tax by making sure the disposal takes place during a tax year in which your taxable income is quite low.

In this respect, company owners can manipulate their incomes more easily than regular employees, sole traders or business partners. The company itself can keep trading and generating profits but the company owner can make sure very little of these profits are extracted and taxed in his or her hands.

Example

Richard, a company owner, sells a buy-to-let property, realising a gain of £50,000 after deducting all buying and selling costs. Deducting his annual CGT exemption of £11,300 leaves a taxable gain of £38,700.

Richard hasn't paid himself any dividends during the current tax year and decides to postpone paying any so that £33,500 of his capital gain is taxed at 18%. The remaining £5,200 will be taxed at 28%. This simple piece of tax planning saves Richard £3,350 in capital gains tax.

Note that Richard can still pay himself a tax-free salary of up to £11,500 to utilise his income tax personal allowance. The income tax personal allowance does not interfere with the capital gains tax calculation. (In practice he may be better off paying himself a slightly smaller salary of £8,164 if his company doesn't have any spare employment allowance.)

Limitations

Although postponing dividends could help you pay less capital gains tax, it's probably not worth doing this unless you can withdraw the postponed dividends in a future tax year and pay no more than 7.5% tax. If you take a bigger dividend in a later tax year, and end up paying 32.5% income tax, you may end up worse off overall.

Example continued

In the above example Richard postponed taking a dividend of £33,500 to free up his basic-rate band and pay 18% capital gains tax.

If during 2018/19 he takes an additional dividend of £33,500, on top off his usual salary and maximum dividend taxed at 7.5%, he will pay additional income tax of £10,888 (£33,500 x 32.5%). However, if he had taken that income in 2017/18 he would have paid income tax of £2,138 – so he ends up paying £8,750 more income tax.

He saved £3,350 in capital gains tax in 2017/18 but pays an additional £8,750 in income tax in 2018/19. Overall Richard is £5,400 worse off.

Part 7

Using a Company: More Tax Benefits & Drawbacks

Chapter 28

Pension Contributions

If you want to make pension contributions there are three main limits you need to know about:

- **The universal limit**. Everyone under 75 can make a pension contribution of £3,600 per year.

- **The earnings limit**. If you want to make bigger pension contributions, you must have *earnings*. For example, if your earnings are £30,000 the maximum pension contribution you can make is £30,000.

- **The annual allowance**. There is also an overall annual limit of £40,000 for contributions made by you and your employer (if you have one). So if your earnings are £60,000, the maximum contribution you (and your employer) can make is £40,000. You can also use any unused allowance from the previous three tax years.

There are further restrictions if your "adjusted income" exceeds £150,000 or you've started withdrawing income from your pension – see the Taxcafe guide *Pension Magic* for more information.

Sole Traders

If you're self-employed your earnings are the pre-tax profits of the business (or your share if the business is a partnership).

For example, a sole trader with pre-tax profits (earnings) of £30,000 can make a pension contribution of £30,000. A sole trader with pre-tax profits of £80,000 can make a pension contribution of £40,000 (restricted by the annual allowance) but possibly £80,000 if he has enough unused allowance from the previous three years.

Company Owners

If you're a company owner your salary counts as earnings but your dividends do not. Dividends are investment income, so you cannot base your pension contributions on them.

A small company owner, taking a tax-free salary of, say, £8,164 during the current tax year, can therefore make a maximum pension contribution of £8,164. This is the *gross* contribution. The company owner would personally invest £6,531 and the taxman would top this up with £1,633 of basic-rate tax relief, producing a total pension contribution of £8,164.

If a company owner wants to make a bigger pension contribution he can, of course, pay himself a bigger salary. However, this could have very unfavourable national insurance consequences. The national insurance on the additional salary could come to 25.8% (12% paid by the company owner, 13.8% paid by the company).

Company Pension Contributions

However, all is not lost. The company owner can get the *company* to make pension contributions on his behalf. Company pension contributions cannot exceed the annual allowance but can exceed your earnings.

Company pension contributions are very tax efficient. The contributions are a tax-deductible expense for the business (i.e. they attract corporation tax relief) and there are no income tax or national insurance consequences for the director or the company.

However, in some cases, there can be a risk that HMRC will deny corporation tax relief if the pension contribution, together with the company owner's other remuneration, amounts to more than a commercial rate of pay for the job they do for the company.

This problem is fairly rare but could affect any company owner who does not play a fully active role in the day to day management of their business.

Should Sole Traders Make Big Contributions?

Although sole traders and other self-employed business owners can make bigger pension contributions than many company owners, this does not mean they should.

If you want to maximise your tax relief, you may wish to restrict the amount you invest. For example, if you have self-employment profits of £50,000 you may wish to make a gross pension contribution no higher than £5,000 (£50,000 - £45,000 higher-rate threshold).

Why? This is the maximum contribution you can make if you want to enjoy higher-rate tax relief (i.e. 40% tax relief) on the entire contribution.

In Scotland the higher-rate threshold is £43,000 so the maximum pension contribution you could make with full higher-rate tax relief would be £7,000 (£50,000 - £43,000).

Summary

- Self-employed business owners (sole traders and partners) often have higher earnings than company owners and can therefore make bigger pension contributions.

- Company owners can get their companies to contribute to their pensions. Company contributions qualify for corporation tax relief and there are no income tax and national insurance consequences.

- However, corporation tax relief on company pension contributions can be denied in certain circumstances so there is arguably less certainty.

Chapter 29

Tax-Free Interest

One of the benefits of being a self-employed business owner, rather than using a company, is you may be able to earn more interest on your business cash. Interest rates on company savings accounts have been decimated in recent years and I've seen rates as low as 0.01% (meaning you earn 1p interest for every £100 in your bank account!)

Sole traders and partners, because they are simply private individuals, can use any savings account and higher interest rates are readily available (although many of the better deals have restrictions or the special interest rate is whipped away after the first year).

Unlike companies, sole traders and partners can also shelter their business cash in a tax-free ISA and it is now possible to withdraw and replace money without it counting towards your annual ISA subscription limit, as long as the repayment is made in the same tax year as the withdrawal.

The New Savings Nil Rate Band

A new savings nil rate band has also been introduced with a 0% tax rate for up to £1,000 of interest income if you're a basic-rate taxpayer and £500 if you're a higher-rate taxpayer. Additional-rate taxpayers cannot benefit from the savings nil rate band.

The automatic deduction of 20% income tax by banks and building societies on non-ISA savings has also been stopped.

The savings nil rate band typically uses up some of your basic-rate band or higher-rate band. For example, if you have £44,500 of self-employment profit and £1,000 of interest income you will have total income of £45,500. With income over £45,000 you will be a higher-rate taxpayer for 2017/18 and entitled to a £500 savings nil rate band. Thus £500 of your interest income will be tax free and this will use up the final £500 of your basic-rate band. The final £500 of interest income will be taxed at 40%.

In summary, thanks to the savings nil rate band and ISAs, many self-employed business owners will be able to earn tax-free interest on their business cash. Companies will continue to pay corporation tax on all their interest income.

The £5,000 Starting Rate Band

Although *companies* may pay more tax on their interest income than sole traders, *company owners* themselves may be able to earn more tax-free interest than sole traders.

As private individuals company owners can benefit from ISAs and the savings nil rate band, just like sole traders. Furthermore, small company owners are more likely to be able to benefit from the *starting rate*, which provides up to £5,000 of tax-free interest each year.

The starting rate is supposed to benefit only those with very low incomes. Hence the £5,000 starting rate band is reduced by any taxable *non-savings* income you have including:

- Employment income
- Self-employment income
- Pension income
- Rental income

If your taxable non-savings income exceeds £5,000, none of your interest income will be tax free under the starting rate.

Most self-employed business owners will have more than £5,000 of taxable non-savings income and therefore cannot benefit from the starting rate band. Many company owners are in a different position, however. Note that the above list of non-savings income does NOT include dividends. Dividends are the top slice of income and do not use up the starting rate band.

Because company owners often pay themselves small salaries and take the rest of their income as dividends, they will often have little or no taxable non-savings income. As a result, many can earn at least £5,000 of tax-free interest!

Example

Mandy is a company owner with a salary of £11,500, dividend income of £28,500 and interest income of £5,000. Her salary is tax free thanks to her personal allowance and she therefore has no taxable non-savings income that uses up her starting rate band (her dividend income does not count). Her interest income is fully covered by her £5,000 starting rate band and taxed at 0%.

Many company owners will thus pay 0% tax on their interest if:

- They take a small salary from their company,
- Do not have a sole trader or partnership business, and
- Don't earn much, if any, rental income.

It is important to point out that the 0% starting rate band is not given in addition to your basic-rate band (£33,500 in 2017/18). Instead it is part of your basic-rate band.

If you qualify to use the starting rate band your basic-rate band will be reduced, possibly pushing some of your dividend income into a higher tax bracket.

Losses

Self-Employed Business Owners

Where a self-employed person's business produces a loss, the general rule is that the loss is carried forward and offset against future profits from the business.

However, losses can also be set off against your **other income** (e.g. from a job or investments) or capital gains from the same tax year or the previous tax year.

This relief is even more generous if you have recently started your business. Losses that arise in the first four tax years of the business can be carried back and offset against your other income from the previous three tax years (earliest year first). In other words, if you start a business and it makes a loss you can claim back tax you've paid in previous years.

The ability to offset losses against your other income and capital gains is extremely valuable. However, the amount you can claim is not unlimited. There is an annual cap on the total amount that can be claimed under this and various other tax reliefs.

The total amount of relief you can claim under all the affected reliefs in any one tax year is limited to the greater of:

- £50,000, or
- 25% of your 'adjusted net income'

Broadly speaking, your adjusted net income is your total taxable income, after deducting gross pension contributions.

The cap does not apply, however, where a loss is set off against earlier profits *from the same trade*.

There are further restrictions for part-time business owners (those spending fewer than 10 hours per week working in the business). The maximum loss relief they can claim is restricted to £25,000.

In summary, if you're self-employed and make a loss you can offset the loss against your other income or capital gains from the same tax year or the previous tax year. Losses that arise in the first four tax years of the business can be carried back and offset against your other income from the previous three tax years.

These reliefs could produce welcome tax repayments. However, there is a limit (£50,000 per year in practice for most individuals) to the total amount of income tax relief that can be claimed.

Company Losses

If your company makes a loss it cannot be offset against your *personal* income. The loss stays inside the company.

Trading losses can be set off against the company's other income and capital gains from the same accounting period.

If the claim to offset trading losses within the same accounting period has been made, the company can also make a claim to carry back any surplus loss against its total profits and capital gains from the previous 12 months.

A loss can only be carried back if the company has already made a claim to first offset the loss against other income and capital gains from the same year.

Carrying the loss back is an attractive option because it will generate a corporation tax repayment.

Any trading losses remaining after any claim to use them in the current or previous year will be carried forward to future years and used as follows:

- Losses arising before 1 April 2017 can be set off against future profits from the *same trade*

- Losses arising since 1 April 2017 can be set off against the company's total income and capital gains, provided that the trade which gave rise to the loss has not ceased or become small or negligible. Where the trade has become small or negligible, the carried forward losses may only be set off against future profits from that trade.

From 1 April 2017 the total amount of relief which a company can claim for carried forward losses is restricted to a maximum of £5 million plus 50% of any profits in excess of that amount.

Summary

If you are starting a business and expect it to make losses initially, the way those losses are treated may influence your decision to set up a company or operate as a sole trader. If you have income from other sources (e.g. a job or investments) your trading losses could result in a tax repayment if you are self employed and this could provide a welcome cash boost at a difficult time.

Chapter 31

Cash Accounting

Sole traders and partnerships with small enough trading businesses can elect to be taxed under the 'cash basis'. Companies and limited liability partnerships (LLPs) are among those who cannot use the cash basis.

Starting on 6 April 2017 the cash basis is now available if the annual turnover of the business does not exceed £150,000. However, once you are using the cash basis you can continue to use it, provided your turnover does not exceed £300,000.

Under the cash basis, income is taxable only when it is received and expenditure is deductible when it is paid. By contrast, under normal accounting principles (known as the accruals basis), income is taxed when it is *earned* and expenses are deductible when they are *incurred*.

The cash basis could be attractive to businesses that have to wait a long time to get paid by their suppliers.

However, businesses that do opt for the simpler cash basis face a number of restrictions.

For example, they are limited to a maximum claim of £500 per year in respect of interest on cash borrowings.

Sideways loss relief is not available, so you cannot offset losses against your other income (see Chapter 30). Losses arising under the cash basis can only be carried forward for set off against future profits from the same trade.

Where the cash basis is used, there is generally no distinction between 'revenue' and 'capital' expenditure. Revenue expenditure includes most of the day to day expenses of a business (e.g. salaries and stationery). Capital expenditure includes purchases of assets that normally qualify for capital allowances.

Under the cash basis capital expenditure can be claimed when it is paid. However, with effect from April 2017, new rules are being introduced which will make it clear that no deduction will be allowed for:

- Non-depreciating assets (generally speaking, those expected to last more than 20 years)
- Assets that aren't for continuing use in the business
- Land (certain property fixtures are allowed)
- Financial assets
- Cars (motoring costs can be claimed in other ways)
- The cost of buying or selling a business
- Capital spending on education and training
- Certain intangible assets (e.g. intellectual property) which last longer than 20 years

Chapter 32

Motoring Costs

Capital Allowances

Cars owned by self-employed business owners and companies enjoy the same capital allowance rates. The size of your capital allowance claim depends on the car's CO_2 emissions, measured in grams of CO_2 per kilometre (g/km):

- Over 130g/km   8% allowance
- Over 75g/km but not over 130g/km   18% allowance
- 75g/km or less   100% allowance

The threshold for the 18% rate will be reduced from 130g/km to 110g/km with effect from 1 April 2018.

The 100% first-year allowance for new low-emission cars has been extended to 31 March 2021, although the qualifying threshold will be reduced from 75g/km to 50g/km from 1 April 2018.

For cars owned by sole traders and partnerships the capital allowance claim is reduced to reflect private use of the vehicle. For example, a car purchased during 2017/18 for £10,000 which has 140g/km of CO_2 emissions and 50% private use will be eligible for an allowance of £400 (8% x £10,000 = £800, less 50%).

For cars owned by companies, there is no restriction in the capital allowance claim for private use. Instead the person who uses the car (e.g. the director) pays income tax on the benefit in kind. The benefit in kind charge will be somewhere between 9% (zero CO_2 emissions) and 37% of the manufacturer's list price. Furthermore, the company will have to pay employer's national insurance at 13.8% on the benefit in kind.

The tax on company cars has been steadily increasing over the years and is only set to get worse. Any business owner who relies on their car for business should be sure to take account of the different tax rules that would apply if they use a company. In some cases, the difference could be enough to make using a company less tax efficient overall.

Selling the Car

A key difference between self-employed businesses and companies is the capital allowance treatment when the car is sold.

Cars owned by sole traders and partnerships are treated as stand-alone assets for capital allowances purposes (provided there is some private use of the vehicle, which there usually is).

This means that, when the car is sold, a balancing allowance is available if the car is sold for less than its tax written down value. This is often the case because most cars lose value at a faster rate than 8% per year!

A balancing allowance essentially makes up for any shortfall in the car's capital allowances. The balancing allowance reduces your taxable profits and therefore reduces your tax bill.

Cars purchased by companies are not treated as separate stand-alone assets. Cars entitled to an 18% writing down allowance are added to the 'general pool' of assets. Cars entitled to an 8% writing down allowance are added to the 'special rate pool' of assets.

This means that, when the car is sold, there will NOT be a big balancing allowance to help reduce the company's tax bill. Instead, the outstanding balance remaining after deducting the car's sale proceeds will continue to attract capital allowances at 8% or 18%, along with other assets inside the pool.

Example

Gordon, a sole trader, buys a car and uses it 75% for business purposes and 25% privately. The car attracts capital allowances of 8% per year. Let's say the car's written down value is currently £25,000.

Gordon then sells the car for just £10,000. This gives rise to a balancing allowance of £11,250:

£25,000 - £10,000 = £15,000
£15,000 x 75% business use = £11,250

This means Gordon can claim a tax deduction of £11,250, saving him £4,725 in tax (at 42%) if he is a higher-rate taxpayer.

This example illustrates one of the key differences between sole traders/partnerships and companies.

Even though Gordon, a sole trader, is only allowed to claim a capital allowance of 8% per year, he can claim a big catch-up tax deduction when he sells the car. He would not be able to claim this balancing allowance if he was using a company. The company would have to continue claiming tax relief at just 8% per year.

Sole traders and partnerships are also not able to claim these big catch-up tax deductions for cars given to their employees or if their own cars have no private use.

Mileage Rates

Company Owners

Company owners who use their own cars for business journeys can receive tax-free business mileage payments from the company (the company can also claim the amount as a tax deduction). Business mileage can be claimed at the following rates:

- 45p per mile (first 10,000 miles)
- 25p per mile thereafter

Many company owners use the mileage rates instead of getting their company to buy a car for their use. This allows them to avoid company car benefit-in-kind tax charges, which are often extremely high. However, for those travelling well over 10,000 miles per year on business, the 25p per mile rate may not provide adequate compensation for the car's depreciation.

Example

Patrick, a company owner, travels 15,000 miles per year on business. He can claim the following tax-free mileage payment from his company:

- *10,000 x 45p = £4,500*
- *5,000   x 25p = £1,250*

Patrick's total tax-free payment for the year will be £5,750. The company can claim the amount as a tax deduction.

Self-Employed Business Owners

Self-employed business owners can also use the above mileage rates and the amount will be allowed as a tax deduction for the business.

The mileage allowances can also be claimed for vans and other goods vehicles and motor cycles (the rate for motor cycles is 24p per mile).

Capital allowances cannot be claimed in addition to the mileage allowances. Furthermore, the mileage rates cannot be used if capital allowances have already been claimed for the vehicle.

As an alternative to the mileage allowances, self-employed business owners can claim capital allowances and their actual motoring costs (fuel, insurance, repairs etc), with a suitable reduction to reflect private use of the vehicle.

The mileage rates may have the advantage of simplicity but which method produces a bigger tax deduction? Sometimes your actual motoring expenses will produce the biggest tax deduction, sometimes the mileage rates – it all depends on your personal circumstances.

The amounts at stake are potentially significant and could amount to thousands of pounds per year. The two most important factors influencing your choice are arguably:

- The cost of your car
- The amount of business mileage

The more expensive your car is, the more important it is to claim capital allowances, which means you will also claim your actual motoring costs.

Chapter 33

Selling Your Business

One of the most tax-efficient ways to grow your wealth is to build and then sell several businesses during your working life.

This allows you to convert streams of heavily taxed income into low-taxed capital gains.

Many self-employed business owners face a marginal tax rate of 42% or more and many company owners face a marginal tax rate of 45% or more (including corporation tax).

But when you sell a business and receive a big cash lump sum, which replaces all this heavily taxed income, you could end up paying less than 10% tax if you qualify for Entrepreneurs Relief.

Up to £10 million of capital gains per person can qualify for Entrepreneurs Relief. This is a lifetime limit but can be used for more than one business sale.

Entrepreneurs Relief can save a couple up to £2 million in capital gains tax, so it's worth knowing what you have to do to protect it.

Sole traders, partnerships and company owners may all potentially qualify but, in each case, the business has to be what the taxman refers to as a 'trade'. Generally speaking this means that investment businesses (e.g. property investment businesses) do not qualify.

Furthermore, to qualify, the business must have been owned for at least one year.

Sole traders are generally only entitled to Entrepreneurs Relief when they sell the whole business (or shut it down and sell off the assets). A part of a business can only qualify if it is capable of operating as a going concern in its own right.

If you continue trading but sell some business assets, for example a piece of intellectual property or your trading premises, you will not be entitled to any Entrepreneurs Relief.

Company Owners

Company owners are entitled to Entrepreneurs Relief when they sell shares in their company. To qualify:

- The company must be your 'personal company', i.e. you must own at least 5% of the ordinary share capital and voting rights

- You must be an officer or employee of the company

- The company must be a 'trading' company

All three of these requirements must be met for at least one year before the business is sold. It does not matter if the requirements are met in earlier years.

Winding Up the Company

It is not always possible to sell your company shares to a third party. Buyers are often fearful of acquiring companies outright for fear of taking on any unknown liabilities. Instead they often prefer to buy the underlying assets (e.g. premises, goodwill, stock and customers).

The disadvantage of an asset sale such as this is the potential double tax charge.

Firstly, your company will pay corporation tax on the proceeds, although indexation relief will be available on certain assets such as property. If you then extract the after-tax proceeds a second tax charge may arise.

The key is making sure the second tax charge is just 10% (thanks to Entrepreneurs Relief) rather than 32.5% or 38.1% (if the distribution is taxed as dividend income).

Providing you meet the qualifying criteria, Entrepreneurs Relief is still available if you wind up your company following an asset sale and extract the cash as a capital distribution.

There are generally two ways to wind up a company:

- Dissolution under the Companies Act
- Voluntary liquidation under the Insolvency Act

With a dissolution capital gains tax treatment is only possible if the total distributions are less than £25,000. Where the total distributions exceed £25,000 they are taxed as dividends, possibly at 32.5% or 38.1%.

A voluntary liquidation, on the other hand, ensures that payments to shareholders can be treated as capital distributions for capital gains tax purposes.

However, voluntary liquidation requires the appointment of a licensed insolvency practitioner with fees running to many thousands of pounds in some cases (the fees may be less if the company's affairs are simple and its main asset is cash).

To qualify for Entrepreneurs Relief the capital distribution must be made within three years of the cessation of trading.

Furthermore, in the 12 months before the cessation of trading the following criteria must be met:

- The company must be your 'personal company', i.e. you must own at least 5% of the ordinary share capital and voting rights

- You must be an officer or employee of the company

- The company must be a 'trading' company

In some cases the existence of a large cash balance (a non-trading asset) may throw in doubt the company owners' ability to claim Entrepreneurs Relief.

It goes without saying that in all cases where a winding up of the company is to be carried out, professional advice should be obtained to ensure the desired tax treatment of the distributions.

TAAR

A new Targeted Anti-Avoidance Rule (TAAR) applying from 6 April 2016 means that, in some cases, profits distributed on a winding up will be treated as dividends. The TAAR has been introduced to prevent company owners having profits taxed at the much lower capital gains tax rates.

The TAAR applies where all of the following conditions are met:

- **Condition A & B**. The company is a close company and the individual holds at least 5% of the ordinary share capital and voting rights

- **Condition C**. Within two years of the distribution the company owner carries on the same or a similar trade or activity to the company being wound up

- **Condition D**. One of the main purposes of the winding up is to reduce income tax, or
  The winding up forms part of arrangements, one of the main purposes of which is to reduce income tax

With regards to Condition C, it makes no difference whether you operate as a sole trader or through a partnership or a new company in which you have at least a 5% interest or through a person with whom you are connected (e.g. your spouse or other close relative).

The test is clearly very subjective and it is feared that it could catch many innocent situations, for example where a company owner retires, winds up his company and a year later decides to take on a few clients or do some work for a family member involved in the same trade.

It is also feared that the third test could be applied broadly. For example, HMRC could argue that if a company owner decides not to pay surplus funds out as dividends prior to the winding up, there is as an 'arrangement' to reduce income tax.

HMRC has provided the following examples which are intended to allay these fears and explain when the new rules will apply:

Example 1

Mr A has been the sole shareholder of a company which carries on the trade of landscape gardening for 10 years. Mr A decides to wind up the business and retire. Because he no longer needs a company he liquidates the company and receives a distribution in a winding up. To subsidise his pension, Mr A continues to do a small amount of gardening in his local village.

Conditions A to C are met, because gardening is a similar trade or activity to landscape gardening. However, when viewed as a whole, these arrangements do not appear to have tax as a main purpose. It is natural for Mr A to have wound up his company because it is no longer needed once the trade has ceased. Although Mr A continues to do some gardening, there is no reason why he would need a company for this, and it does not seem that he set the company up, wound it up and then continued a trade all with a view to receive the profits as capital rather than income. In these circumstances, Mr A's distribution in the winding up will continue to be treated as capital.

Example 2

Mrs B is an IT contractor. Whenever she receives a new contract, she sets up a limited company to carry out that contract. When the work is completed and the client has paid, Mrs B winds up the company and receives the profits as capital.

Again, conditions A to C are met because Mrs B has a new company which carries on the same or a similar trade to the previously wound up company. Here, though, it looks like there is a main purpose of obtaining a tax advantage. All of the contracts could have been operated through the same company, and apart from the tax savings it would seem that would have been the most sensible option for Mrs B. Where the distribution from the winding up is made on or after 6 April 2016, in these circumstances the distribution will be treated as a dividend and subject to income tax.

Example 3

Mrs C is an accountant who has operated through a limited company for three years. She decides that the risk involved with running her own business is not worth her effort, and so decides to accept a job at her brother's accountancy firm as an employee. Her brother's firm has been operating for eight years. Mrs C winds up her company and begins life as an employee.

Conditions A to C are met because Mrs C is continuing a similar activity to the trade that was carried on by the company. She is continuing it as an employee of a connected party, triggering Condition C. But looking at the arrangements as a whole it is not reasonable to assume that they have tax advantage as a main purpose, so Condition D will not be met. Mrs C's company was incorporated and wound up for commercial, not tax, reasons; although she works for a connected party it is clear that the other business was not set up to facilitate a tax advantage because it has been operating for some time. In these circumstances, the distribution from the winding up will continue to be treated as capital, absent any other considerations.

The Targeted Anti-Avoidance Rule is not the only risk company owners face when they liquidate their company. HMRC can also use the "Transaction in Securities" legislation to tax liquidation distributions as dividends if it believes the winding up is mainly driven by income tax avoidance.

There is uncertainty amongst tax professionals as to how this measure will be applied in practice and so many recommend obtaining advance clearance from HMRC before a winding up takes place.

Because the various anti-avoidance rules cast doubt over how profits distributed in a winding up will be taxed, it may also make sense to pay actual dividends over the course of a few tax years, rather than making a single large distribution when you wind up the company.

Adopting a phased approach to the withdrawal of profits from your company may allow you to enjoy the 7.5% tax rate that applies to basic-rate taxpayers, rather than the 32.5% or 38.1% tax rates that apply to higher and additional-rate taxpayers. Adopting this strategy over several tax years could allow a significant amount of cash to be extracted from the company, especially when the amounts taxed at 7.5% can be doubled up in the case of a company owned by a couple.

Final Tax Planning Pointers

Beware of Incorporating

If you have a sole trader business or partnership, you should be wary of incorporating (putting the business into a company) within one year of selling. To qualify for Entrepreneurs Relief, you have to own the shares of the newly formed company for at least one year.

Be Wary of Business Transfers to Family Members

Transfers to spouses are exempt from CGT and can save significant amounts of income tax. However, if the business is sold less than one year after the transfer, Entrepreneurs Relief will not be available on the transferred share unless the spouse already held a share of the business before that (and for at least a year prior to the sale).

Chapter 34

Business Property

Self Employed

Many sole traders own their own premises (offices, shops, warehouses etc). They can't pay themselves rent but many of their property expenses (e.g. mortgage interest, repairs, insurance etc) are all allowed as a tax deduction against the profits of the business, allowing the sole trader to pay less income tax and national insurance.

Business partners can rent property to the partnership. Charging the partnership rent will reduce the taxable profits of the business and allow the partners to receive rental income which avoids national insurance.

If the property is sold for a profit, capital gains tax may be payable at either 10% (basic-rate taxpayers) or 20% (higher-rate taxpayers). These are the new lower capital gains tax rates applying to *non-residential* property from 6 April 2016.

Business owners may also qualify for two special CGT reliefs:

- Rollover Relief
- Entrepreneurs Relief

Rollover Relief can be claimed if you move to different trading premises. Effectively it lets you postpone paying capital gains tax on the old property until the new property is sold. This gives the business flexibility to grow without adverse tax consequences.

You can buy the new property between a year before and three years after selling the original property. All of the old property's sale proceeds must be reinvested. Any shortfall is deducted from the amount of gain eligible for rollover. Relief is also restricted if there is less than full trading use of the property.

Entrepreneurs Relief allows you to pay capital gains tax at just 10%. However, it can generally only be claimed as part of an overall sale of the business.

Company Owners

Business properties can be owned by either:

- The company
- The company owner

If the property belongs to the company owner, the company can pay him rent. Provided the rent is not excessive, the company will enjoy corporation tax relief on these rent payments.

Paying rent is not mandatory but is often tax efficient if the company owner has tax-deductible expenses (e.g. mortgage interest) that can be offset against the rental income. Rent has also become more attractive following the increase in dividend tax.

Charging rent will, however, reduce the amount of Entrepreneurs Relief you can claim (see below).

Selling the Property

The good news is Entrepreneurs Relief is available when business premises owned *personally* by a company owner are sold as part of the sale of the business, although there are a number of conditions that have to be met.

The bad news is that many business owners will not qualify for the maximum tax relief when "associated" assets like these are sold.

Rent covering any period after 5 April 2008 restricts your entitlement to Entrepreneurs Relief. The taxman's reasoning is that if the property is only available if rent is paid, it is an investment asset and not a business asset.

There are two pieces of good news here, however. Firstly, any rent receivable before April 2008 is disregarded and, secondly, rent paid at less than the market rate only leads to a partial reduction in the available Entrepreneurs Relief.

What happens if the company owns the property? If the buyer of the business wants the property included in the sale, you could sell your shares in the company and all of the proceeds may qualify for Entrepreneurs Relief.

However, an expensive property asset may put off prospective buyers who don't need it (e.g. if the business being sold is not reliant on a specific property – think internet company rather than restaurant). The property may then have to be sold first with corporation tax payable on the capital gain and income tax paid when the money is extracted from the company prior to the sale.

Stand-alone Sales

What if there is a stand-alone sale of the property and no Rollover Relief claim (because the proceeds are not used to buy another property) and no Entrepreneurs Relief claim (because the business is not being sold)?

Individuals who are higher-rate taxpayers now pay up to 20% capital gains tax when they sell non-residential property and 28% when they sell residential property.

Companies currently pay corporation tax at 19% but this will fall to 17% in April 2020.

So if you are a higher-rate taxpayer, your company may eventually pay less tax than you would.

The first £11,300 of an individual's capital gains are tax free thanks to the annual exemption. Companies instead enjoy indexation relief which is potentially much more valuable. For a property costing £250,000, indexation relief could shelter around £50,000 of the gain from tax if the property is sold in 10 years' time, providing inflation averages around 2% per year.

Inheritance Tax

Shares in private trading companies or the value of a partnership interest in a trade or profession are generally exempt from inheritance tax.

A property held personally but used by such a company or partnership, only attracts 50% relief, leaving inheritance tax payable at an effective rate of 20% on the property's value.

Non-tax Factors

- **Insolvency**. As a company owner, one of the benefits of holding your business premises personally is that, if the company becomes insolvent, a property owned by the director personally should be safe from creditors (unless fraud or negligence is involved).

- **Mortgages**. You may find it more difficult to find an attractive mortgage deal if the property is owned by your company.

- **Retirement**. Many company owners view the business premises as their pension – available to rent to their old company or another business after they retire.

Chapter 35

Borrowing Money

New companies sometimes struggle to raise finance. However, it's important to point out that, as a company owner, you can borrow money *personally* and invest it or lend it to your company and personally claim tax relief on the interest.

You can claim tax relief for the interest you pay as a deduction against *any* taxable income you have, e.g. salary income, dividends and interest.

For example, a company owner could borrow against their home, lend the money to their company and all of the interest can be claimed against the company owner's taxable income from all sources.

This tax deduction is known as 'qualifying loan interest'.

Qualifying loan interest may allow you to enjoy tax relief at 40% if you are a higher-rate taxpayer. By contrast, companies currently enjoy no more than 19% corporation tax relief on their interest charges.

Example

Guy, a higher-rate taxpayer, borrows money personally and lends it to his company. Guy's interest bill on the borrowed funds comes to £10,000. Guy also has income of £20,000 from other sources. His interest bill can be set off against this income, resulting in an income tax saving of £4,000 (£10,000 x 40%).

If the company itself borrowed the money, it would only enjoy corporation tax relief of £1,900 (£10,000 x 19%).

Qualifying Loan Interest – Who Can Use It?

There are some restrictions on who can benefit from this tax relief:

- The borrowing company must be a close company, i.e. under the control of five people or less. Most private companies are close companies.

- The investor must generally own 5% or more of the company's share capital. Shares owned by close family members are usually counted but you must own at least some shares yourself.

- The company must carry on a qualifying activity, which typically means carrying on a trade on a commercial basis or letting properties to unconnected third parties.

There is also an annual limit on the total amount of income tax relief available from this tax relief and certain other reliefs. The total amount of relief is limited to the *greater* of:

- £50,000, or
- 25% of your 'adjusted total income'

Drawbacks

One of the dangers of borrowing money personally is that personal debts are not protected by the company's limited liability status. In practice, however, most banks insist on personal guarantees from small company directors anyway, so either way you will probably be personally exposed if you borrow money for your company.

Another problem with borrowing money personally is that you may not have enough personal income from other sources to service the debt.

For example, if the money you borrow is *invested* in your company (ie used to buy shares in your company), you may have to declare a dividend to service the personal debt. If income tax is payable on the dividend, this will eliminate the tax benefit of obtaining personal interest relief.

Lending Money to Your Company

Instead of investing the money in your company you can lend it to your company. Your company can pay you interest if this is required to service your personal debt.

This income will be taxable, although company owners can often enjoy at least £5,000 of tax-free interest (see Chapter 29).

The company will be able to claim corporation tax relief on the interest, provided a commercial rate of interest is charged. If you do this, the company is required to deduct basic-rate tax and account for it to HMRC. The company owner can, however, reclaim it at a later date when they complete their own tax return.

It is often worth charging the maximum market rate applying because interest income can be more tax efficient than salaries or dividends.

One benefit of lending money to your company, as opposed to investing it, is that the money can be withdrawn at a later date with no adverse tax consequences.

Part 8

Incorporating & Disincorporating an Existing Business

Chapter 36

Incorporating an Existing Business

Although it's relatively cheap and easy to set up a company, incorporating an *existing* sole trader business or partnership is more complicated and costly.

The additional costs – professional adviser fees and tax charges – have to be weighed against the ongoing tax savings you hope to achieve from using a company.

It is essential to obtain professional advice before incorporating an existing business.

One important issue is getting the goodwill of the business valued correctly. HMRC has been known to look at goodwill valuations carefully to make sure they can be commercially justified.

This chapter contains a brief overview of some incorporation tax issues.

Capital Gains Tax (CGT)

Capital gains tax is often an important issue for businesses seeking to incorporate. The main assets affected are goodwill and property (although many business owners prefer to keep their property, e.g. their business premises, *outside* the company).

When assets like goodwill and property are transferred from you to your company the transfer is treated as having taken place at market value, which means CGT may be payable.

CGT can be handled in one of three ways:

- Paying the tax in full
- Using Incorporation Relief
- Using Holdover Relief

Paying CGT in Full

Up until fairly recently, thanks to Entrepreneurs Relief, individuals and partnerships incorporating their trading businesses paid just 10% capital gains tax on the goodwill transferred to their company. The company could also claim corporation tax relief on this goodwill, which could significantly reduce the tax payable on its profits over a number of years.

Unfortunately sole traders and partnerships can no longer enjoy Entrepreneurs Relief when they transfer goodwill to their company. Furthermore, corporation tax relief on the amortisation of goodwill has also been stopped.

Although Entrepreneurs Relief is no longer available on goodwill transfers, it's worth noting that the main rates of capital gains tax have been reduced from 6 April 2016 as follows:

- From 18% to 10%   Basic-rate taxpayers
- From 28% to 20%   Higher-rate taxpayers

(Note, these new reduced rates do not apply to disposals of residential property.)

Thus if a sole trader who is a higher-rate taxpayer transfers £100,000 of goodwill to his company the first £11,300 will be tax free (thanks to the annual CGT exemption) and the remaining £88,700 will be taxed at 20%, producing a total tax bill of £17,740.

Typically with these transactions the company will pay for the goodwill by crediting the director's loan account. So if £100,000 of goodwill is transferred to the company, the director can withdraw £100,000 tax free from the company in the future (although it may be more tax-efficient to take a small tax-free salary and low-taxed dividend first).

The company can also pay the director interest on the loan account. The interest will be a tax deductible expense for the company and possibly tax free in the hands of the director thanks to the £5,000 starting rate band (see Chapter 29).

Although Entrepreneurs Relief is no longer available on goodwill transfers it is still available when business property is transferred to a company.

Incorporation Relief

Thanks to Incorporation Relief it is possible to transfer the goodwill and other chargeable assets such as business property to the company without an immediate CGT charge.

However, this is potentially a very restrictive tax relief because to qualify:

- All of the assets of the business (excluding cash if desired) must be transferred to the company, and

- The business must be transferred as a going concern, and

- The business must be transferred wholly or partly in exchange for shares issued by the company to the person transferring the business.

The capital gain arising from the transfer of the assets is deducted from the individual's base cost in the company shares.

The capital gains are deferred and only crystallise when the company owner disposes of his shares.

Incorporation Relief is given automatically and no claim is required. However, it is possible to make an election for the relief to not apply.

Technically, this relief should be available whenever any 'business' is transferred to a company wholly or partly in exchange for shares.

A huge area of difficulty arises, however, in determining exactly what constitutes a 'business' for this purpose. Certainly, anything that may be deemed to be a 'trade' would qualify but beyond this matters become unclear. There is no statutory definition of what constitutes a business for the purposes of Incorporation Relief.

Many residential landlords are looking to use Incorporation Relief to avoid CGT when they incorporate their property businesses. For a full discussion of this issue see the Taxcafe guide *Using a Property Company to Save Tax*.

Holdover Relief (Gift Relief)

Holdover Relief can be claimed as an alternative to Incorporation Relief. The advantage of this relief is that you do not have to transfer all of the assets into the company. Some assets can be kept outside the company.

The relief works by allowing the capital gain on the transfer to be 'held over'. This means that the individual making the transfer has no capital gains tax to pay but it also means that the assets transferred to the company have a lower base cost. The assets' base cost is reduced by the amount of gain held over.

Unlike Incorporation Relief, with this relief the *company* becomes responsible for tax when the asset is eventually sold.

Note that this relief is not automatic and a claim must be made jointly by the transferring taxpayer and the recipient company.

Example

Manos runs his e-commerce business from an office in Manchester. He decides to transfer the business, including the office which he owns personally, into a new company called Manos Manchester Ltd.

He bought the office for £200,000. Its current market value is £500,000. Manos decides to gift the property to Manos Manchester Ltd.

Normally Manos would have a capital gain of £300,000. However, if Manos and his company jointly elect to hold over the gain, Manos will not have to pay any capital gains tax. Manos Manchester Ltd will hold the property with a base cost of £200,000:

Market value	*£500,000*
Less: Gain held over	*£300,000*
Base cost	*£200,000*

The company ends up with the same base cost as the individual. If the company sells the property eventually it will pay corporation tax on the capital gain (calculated using a £200,000 base cost).

Rather than gifting assets like trading premises for no consideration, another option is to sell them to the company. This may result in capital gains tax being payable but in many cases the individual will be entitled to Entrepreneurs Relief (10% capital gains tax).

The company can pay for the property by crediting the director's loan account. This amount can then be withdrawn tax free later on (i.e. with no income tax or national insurance).

For higher-rate taxpayers, paying 10% capital gains tax may be more attractive than the tax payable on salaries and dividends.

Other business owners prefer to retain *personal* ownership of their trading premises. This allows them to receive rental income payments from the company and protects the property from commercial risks (i.e. creditors) and protects them from paying stamp duty land tax.

Personal ownership of trading premises has drawbacks too. For example, if the company is sold, where rent has been paid by the company to the company owner, the amount of Entrepreneurs Relief available for the property will be restricted (possibly no relief will be allowed if a full market rent has been paid). For inheritance tax purposes only 50% business property relief is allowed for properties owned personally.

Stamp Duty Land Tax (SDLT)

If you are a sole trader and decide to transfer your trading premises to your company, the transfer may be subject to stamp duty land tax (Land and Buildings Transaction Tax in Scotland). This tax is payable even if the property is transferred for no consideration because the company and the sole trader are treated as connected persons. In other words, the company is deemed to have paid the market value for the property for stamp duty purposes.

Although there is no stamp duty on goodwill, some property-based businesses may see the value of their transferred properties increased for stamp duty land tax purposes to reflect the inherent goodwill attaching to the property (i.e. the goodwill that arises from the location of the property).

Many business owners prefer to keep the property outside the company, owning it personally and leasing it to the company instead. Stamp duty land tax may still be payable if there is a formal lease. However, in many cases SDLT can be avoided by granting the company a non-exclusive licence to occupy the property.

Where a partnership or limited liability partnership (LLP) is incorporated it may be possible to transfer properties without any SDLT charge. To obtain the exemption, the company needs to be 'connected' with one or more of the partners. If it is 'connected' with all/both of the partners, complete exemption is possible.

The good news is that a company will generally be 'connected' with all/both of the partners if all/both of those partners are:

- Spouses or civil partners,
- Siblings, or
- Parents and their adult children

And these individuals also own the company.

Hence, the most obvious example is where a married couple have been running a business as a partnership and they transfer the business to their own company.

VAT

If the business is VAT registered the company will also need to be registered for VAT.

VAT would normally be chargeable on many of the assets and goodwill transferred to the company. However, if a business is transferred as a going concern the supply is normally outside the scope of VAT.

An election can be made using form VAT68 to transfer the existing VAT number to the company. This results in the VAT rights and duties of the previous business being transferred to the company.

VAT issues also need to be considered when commercial property is transferred to a company. Where the owner has exercised the option to tax (to charge VAT on rent so that VAT can be recovered on expenses), the company may need to make a fresh option to tax before the transfer takes place so that the going concern rules can be used to avoid VAT being charged on the transfer.

Capital Allowances

When the company takes over assets on which capital allowances have been claimed a joint election can be made to transfer the assets at their written down value.

Capital allowances are a complex area and professional advice may be necessary.

Chapter 37

Disincorporation Relief

What if you already own a company but want to run your business as a sole trader or partnership?

As we've shown throughout this guide, using a company can produce worthwhile tax savings... but not always. And companies are potentially more time consuming and costly to run.

To help trading companies avoid the tax charges that arise when they convert to sole trader or partnership status the Government introduced a tax relief called Disincorporation Relief, which runs out on 31 March 2018.

Take up has been very low, with the Office of Tax Simplification reporting fewer than 50 applications to date! This may be due to the very low qualifying limit of £100,000 of assets. This rules out most companies that own any properties or have accumulated goodwill.

The Office of Tax Simplification is currently gathering views to see if improvements can be made to the relief so that a better version may be introduced when the existing one expires.

How it Works

To qualify:

- The business must be transferred as a going concern
- All the assets must be transferred (except cash)
- The total market value of the goodwill and property must not exceed £100,000
- All the shareholders must be individuals
- All the shareholders must have held their shares for the 12 months before the transfer

The claim must be made jointly by the company and all the shareholders.

This allows the assets to be transferred at a reduced value (e.g. the original purchase price of a building) so that no corporation tax is paid by the company.

However, tax is not avoided, it is simply postponed. The shareholders who then receive the company's assets will inherit the reduced transfer value for capital gains tax purposes which means tax may be payable if the assets are eventually sold.

Lightning Source UK Ltd.
Milton Keynes UK
UKOW01f2041191017
311295UK00004B/210/P